FRESH EXPRESSIONS
OF THE RURAL CHURCH

Michael Adam Beck
and
Tyler Kleeberger

FRESH EXPRESSIONS
OF THE RURAL CHURCH

Abingdon Press
Nashville

FRESH EXPRESSIONS OF THE RURAL CHURCH

LCCN has been requested.

ISBN: 978-1-7910-2579-3

MANUFACTURED IN THE UNITED STATES OF AMERICA

Contents

Contents

Start Digging Here

Whatever has happened—that's what will happen again;
whatever has occurred—that's what will occur again.
There's nothing new under the sun. (Ecclesiastes 1:9)

At the simplest level, every harvest results from the interaction between a seed and the soil. A seed has all the potential for life coded inside, but it must be placed in an environment conducive to growth. It's this relationship between seeds and the cumulative factors such as soil, topography, and climate, that lead to a crop.

So we begin by getting some dirt beneath our fingernails while we dig into the soils of the rural context in the United States. For this, we need a soil map.

Soil maps are typically used for land evaluation, agricultural planning, or environmental protection. Soil maps can display primary soil attributes or secondary soil information, such as the properties of the soils. These maps can be helpful in determining the potential soil use: soil production capacity, reaction to certain crops, soil functions, soil degradation measures, and so on.

Before cultivating a piece of land for some specific purpose, a soil map is of vital importance. Similarly, before rotating ministry crops in rural congregations, or before ploughing, harrowing, and seeding new forms of

Christian community in our parish, we need a good soil map to understand the landscape in which we are working.

It's challenging to develop a good soil map of rural congregations across the United States. It would require thousands of soil maps, for every rural congregation is as unique as the context where it is situated and the people who call it home.

A book that explores faithful, fruitful, and innovative ways to go about rural ministry by only examining the condition of the soil today would be a half-hearted effort. We find it necessary to begin by turning over the uppermost soil of rural America to bring fresh nutrients to the surface. In the process we will need to bury some weeds and decaying crop remnants, so they can become fertilizer later.

Where did the rural church come from? Perhaps having a clear answer to this question can help us act accordingly in the present and chart a course to a fruitful future. We must avoid a myopic view of history. We must also avoid pushing the dreadful acts of that history under the rug.

At the deepest level of US American soil is an entire history of indigenous people. Scholars debate the details of how these people arrived, perhaps across the Bering Strait during the most recent Ice Age. Nevertheless, we do know with great certainty that various tribes migrated from the north to the south and occupied these lands for at least 20,000 years. Hence, Europeans arrived in what was to them a "new world," but for the indigenous population, this was the land they called simply *home*. These native inhabitants are people of sophisticated, mature cultures and religions. They share a rich tapestry of established languages. Much work is yet to be done in exploring the treasury of gifts they've offered to the world.

For US Americans, the deepest level of our soil sample is *soaked with blood*. The first settlers of our rural communities were not white, and we need to be honest that our ancestry didn't begin with "us"; nor was the takeover of land done in a way reflective of our Christian teachings. The treatment of these indigenous peoples is a sad and dark legacy of our nation, and one that is important for us rural people to acknowledge and make amends for. As we will show later, no one is more suited for that work than rural congregations.

By scanning the furthest reaches of history, we better understand where we are, including the messy story of how we got to our current place. To cultivate innovative and multiplying faith communities in the rural context, exploring every layer of soil is important. Ploughing here may turn over some fresh nutrients in which to plant new organisms in the present century.

Nathan Hatch is a leading scholar on issues related to the history of religion in the United States. In *The Democratization of American Christianity*, Hatch writes, "The democratic religious movements of the early republic all took root in the same soil, an environment that favored certain approaches, answers, and leadership styles."[1]

To understand the context of the rural church in the United States today, we take a sample from the century-long period between the American Revolution and the Civil War (approximately 1765 to 1861).

This soil stratum in the religious landscape of rural America is *scorched with fire*.

Barnstorming the Backcountry

Circuit riders (Methodist and Baptist) crisscrossed what was for them a new frontier, planting churches across the landscape of the United States. They shared the story of Jesus with whomever would listen, leaving in their wake constellations of new Christian communities, the majority located in rural areas. These ministers burned with the zeal of enthusiasm, dissent, and a commitment to form new Christian communities in the most remote places of the far-flung terrain.

Before 1800, this lament from an Episcopal preacher was typical of an elite leader: "How many thousands . . . never saw, much less read, or ever heard a chapter of the Bible! How many Ten thousands never were baptized or heard a sermon! And thrice Ten thousand, who never heard the Name of Christ, save in Curses!"[2]

But then, reports from across the field in the spring of 1802 described a religious awakening that was "spreading along like a moving fire."[3] This sweeping revival led Charles Finney to refer to western New York state, an area particularly active with emerging insurgent groups, as the "burnt district."[4] Meaning, the region was so set ablaze with spiritual fervor it was left smoldering.

Who were these apostles, lit aflame by the fires of revival? What kind of communities can we find in this layer of ash? How might this be fresh fertilizer for today?

We do know that the congregations left in their fiery wake became the centerpiece of rural life, for a time. In these places people gathered not only to hear a sermon on Sundays but also to help one another work the land, break bread, and form deep relationships. The rural church was the place where they found a community that could sustain them through the joys and struggles of life with the land. In many ways, the rural church captured a core essence of the church's mission: to be the guiding hand to the life of a place.

Jeffrey Williams acknowledges some debate as to what level these insurgent Christian movements shaped the "American mind." Did these Christian trailblazers provide the content, inspiration, and structures for colonists to imagine a new political entity birthed through revolution? Revivalism, at least indirectly, fueled the revolution by establishing structures and new patterns of leadership, communication, and public participation that bred and sustained resistance to traditional authority.[5]

To understand the formation of rural culture in the United States, and its rich contributions to culture today, we examine these insurgent expressions of church.

In Hatch's examination of the religious history of the early republic and the enduring structures of American Christianity, he focuses primarily on leaders and movements between 1780 and 1830. He poses questions about the relationship between these leaders and their constituents, to identify themes that are common to a variety of religious groups.[6]

In the wake of the revolution for independence, individualism, dissent, and democracy became ideals taken up into a new iteration of American Christianity. A group of insurgent leaders—Methodist, Baptist, Christian, Universalist, Disciple, Millerite, and Mormon—arose and sought to catalyze a movement toward new forms of church among ordinary people. Hatch observes, "They shared an ethic of unrelenting toil, a passion for expansion, a hostility to orthodox belief and style, a zeal for religious reconstruction, and a systematic plan to realize their ideals" and perhaps most notable, "they all offered common people, especially the poor, compelling visions of individual self-respect and collective self-confidence." Each of these emergent leaders was also highly skilled in communication and group mobilization.[7]

A common theme among these religious groups and their leaders is an impulse toward democratization, which "has less to do with the specifics of polity and governance and more with the incarnation of the church into popular culture."[8] Hatch lists three key ways these movements articulated a democratic spirit:

- First, they denied the clergy/laity distinction.

- Second, they empowered ordinary people.

- Third, they held an audacious belief that authoritarian structures would be overthrown.[9]

These movements played a role in unleashing a vast transformation, a "shift away from enlightenment and classical republicanism toward vulgar democracy and materialistic individualism," this was "the real American Revolution."[10] These religious leaders used and popularized print media, changing the very character of the medium in the process of furthering their movements. Just consider between 1790 and 1810, the United States witnessed an explosion in the growth of newspapers, from 90 to 370.[11] In essence, these movements created alternative systems of communication outside the conventional channels.

The fundamental religious quarrel of the late-eighteenth century was not between theological positions but was a radically different conception of the Christian ministry. Emerging leaders raced to erase the distinction between gentleman and commoner, between privileged classes and the people.[12] William Bentley (1759–1819), minister of the East Church in Salem, Massachusetts, groaned, "The people were doing theology for themselves."[13]

These insurgent movements took place amid a massive population increase. While the population of the United States was less than half of England's in 1775, by 1845, Americans outnumbered the English by five million. This population boom was overwhelmingly rural. The ratio of people to land barely doubled while the population expanded tenfold. In 1970, 94 percent of the population lived in the thirteen colonies; by 1850, only half the population did.[14]

American Christianity was a fire in the fields, a barnstorm in the backcountry.

This firestorm was in part due to the impotence and disarray of the established Congregational, Presbyterian, and Episcopalian churches. Membership was dwindling in these congregations. Fewer young men were entering the ministry. Those who did came from upper-class families, were educated at Harvard and Yale, and were less open to serving in the hardship of a backcountry parish with low pay.[15] To give a snapshot of this reality, consider that in 1816 there were twelve Episcopal clergymen on the entire Delmarva Peninsula (which consists of most of Delaware, parts of the Eastern Shore regions of Maryland, and Virginia), competing with thirty Methodist itinerants and two hundred local preachers.[16]

A host of emerging popular leaders stepped forward to light the rural landscape on fire with a democratized Christianity: Henry Alline, Alexander Campbell, John Leland, Barton Stone, William Miller, Lorenzo Dow,

Peter Cartwright, Joseph Smith, and more. Waves of women and persons of color became converts during this time and took leadership of the movement in new and revolutionary ways. Harry Hosier, Richard Allen, Barbara Heck, Ellen Gould White, Jarnea Lee, Sojourner Truth, Phoebe Palmer, and many others began laying the foundation for women's rights, temperance, and abolition.

Each of these movements shaped the rural landscape in incalculable ways. Perhaps, no movement more fully captures the spirit of these times and explains the rural congregational soil conditions we have inherited today like that of Francis Asbury and the American Methodists.

From the Center to the Circumference

John Wigger writes:

Francis Asbury lived one of the most remarkable lives in American history, a life that many have admired and few have envied. The son of an English gardener, he became one of America's leading religious voices and the person most responsible for shaping American Methodism. Through sheer perseverance and dedication to a single goal, he changed American popular religion—and by extension American culture—as much as anyone ever has. America is one of the most religious nations on earth, and Asbury is an important reason why.[17]

Hatch probes the understated and understudied nature of this insurgent movement. His research reveals it was Methodism, exceedingly more than Puritanism, that explained the distinct character of religious life in the United States. He argues that, "quite simply, Methodism remains the most powerful religious movement in American history, its growth a central feature in the emergence of the United States as a republic."[18]

Hatch outlines how a fledgling American Methodism had merely four ministers and 300 laypeople in 1771, almost went extinct during the Revolution, and then exploded with growth into the hundreds of thousands following. Methodist leaders returned to England at the beginning of the war, leaving a lone, British twenty-something-year-old Francis Asbury to continue the work on the continent.[19]

John Wesley was not a pacifist. He held to a version of just-war theory and even took a position against the United States in the Revolutionary War. For Wesley, loyalty to God was loyalty to the crown. Wesley described the American desire for independence as unlawful, and even condemned colonists as a band of immoral and unrighteous sinners undermining the divinely established monarchy. Meanwhile, Asbury and the American Methodists took a position of passivity and in large part tried to remain neutral regarding the war.[20]

Asbury spread the movement from Canada to Georgia, with an army of uneducated preachers, organized in local cells and preaching circuits. By the time Asbury died in 1816, Methodism had over 2,000 ministers and 200,000 Methodist members. Between 1776 and 1850, American Methodists grew from less than 3 percent of all US church members to more than 34 percent. They became unequivocally the largest religious body in the nation. By the mid-nineteenth century, Methodists had grown to 4,000 itinerants, almost 8,000 local preachers, and over a million members. It was almost double the size of any other Protestant body and boasted of ten times the preaching force of the Congregationalists, who in 1776 had double the number of clergy than any other church.[21]

Wigger notes that the typical itinerant rode a predominantly rural circuit of 200 to 500 miles, averaging twenty-five to thirty preaching appointments per round. They completed the circuit every two to six weeks with the standard being a four weeks' circuit of 400 miles. Asbury's American adaptation of this itinerant system seemed custom designed for the expanding rural frontier.[22]

The Methodist system of organization was entirely mobile. "Itineration," the key to the strategy, consisted of ministers and leaders, traveling from place to place. It was unique in that Methodists did not have "pastors in residence" charged to care for a single flock. By necessity, laity stepped into positions of shared leadership. In the cities, the congregations were organized as "stations" or a network of faith communities. Preachers in the cities circulated among various congregations, preaching three services on Sunday alone (morning, afternoon, and evening). The participants in these gatherings would hear a different preacher every service.

In the country, circuits consisted of networks of congregations spread across vast distances. Sometimes they met in barns, houses, fields, or crossroads. If you've ever traveled throughout a particularly unpopulated countryside but noticed old Methodist church buildings every five to ten miles, it's probably the surviving network from early circuits. In many cases, the first communal and permanent structures built in rural locations were these churches. Methodists earned the title "Church of the Horse,"[23] and the backcountry was their parish. These circuit riders, and the local preachers and exhorters that helped them, played a role in shaping the American countryside that we have inherited today.

Wigger notes, "While Methodism retained a stronghold in the seaports of the middle states, Asbury hammered its organization into one that had a distinctly rural orientation adept at expanding into newly populated areas."[24]

Asbury wrote in 1797, "We must draw resources from the centre to the circumference."[25]

Asbury saw that the primary calling of Methodists was to the rural places. He had a particular cultural sensitivity and could see the potential for Methodism outside the urban centers. Hatch describes this as a "strategic advantage in the free-religious economy of a westward-moving nation which was increasingly suspicious of the pretensions of educated professionals-lawyers, physicians, and clergy men."[26]

While the Methodists had very few college-educated clergy among their thousands of circuit riders and local preachers, Congregational (one forerunner to the UCC) ministers were educated at Yale, Harvard, and Dartmouth. Those ministers made a choice to serve the more populated and "civilized" areas. Methodists, Baptists, and other insurgent forms of Christianity, flourished in rural places.[27]

In several ways, American Methodism veered sharply away from the course of British Methodism.[28] It brought together the explosive conjunction of evangelical fervor and popular sovereignty (government for and by the will of the people), which allowed "indigenous expressions of faith to take hold among ordinary people, white and black." This allowed Christianity to be effectively reshaped by common people.[29] In turn, this became a staple of not only rural churches but rural communities.

This mix shattered class barriers and empowered everyday believers to explore a call to ministry. It challenged the prominent ecclesiastical hierarchy, promoted autonomy, and tapped into the subversive spirit of the American people. It also broke free from the mold of Eurotribal Christianity. While British Methodism was deeply committed to abolishing slavery, Black persons actually found a spiritual home in American Methodism. Hatch states, "More African Americans became Christians in ten years of Methodist preaching than in a century of Anglican influence."[30]

Hatch notes that Asbury and company emphasized three themes that Americans found captivating: "God's free grace, the liberty of people to accept or reject that grace, and the power and validity of popular religious expression-even among servants, women, and African Americans."[31] Much of American Methodism's early growth came from Black persons. From 1790 to 1810, one-fifth of Methodist membership was comprised of Black Americans.[32]

As we will explore in depth, these insurgent movements became the seeds of the Black church in the United States, and the rapid expansion of the Methodist movement escalated tensions between the North and South, leading to the Civil War.

New People, New Places, New Ways

Stephen Webb noted that American Methodism took John Wesley's innovations a step further. Wesley took the gospel to those on the edge of established religion, by delivering passionate sermons in the fields that emphasized personal rather than institutional expressions of faith.[33] Since vast tracts of land were sparsely settled, and educated clergy were in short supply, American Methodism depended even more on lay preaching. Weeping, shouting, and groaning were common at these services, leading some to refer to Methodist gatherings as "wild and messy."[34] The converted were encouraged to participate in revival meetings where "passion was more important than doctrine."[35]

Where field preaching was a primary tool for Wesley, the campmeeting in rural spaces was a primary tool for American Methodists.

"Campmeetings! Campmeetings! The battle ax and weapon of war, it will break down walls of wickedness, part of hell, superstition, [and] false doctrine!"[36] said Asbury. Thomas Coke and British Methodist leaders disapproved of campmeetings.[37] Yet, these gatherings were instrumental in catalyzing the first "mixed race" congregations.

Campmeetings not only facilitated conversion but also radically democratized social relationships. People once excluded from public authority—persons of color, women, slaves, and the unlearned—now claimed leadership alongside those with positions of power. The gatherings also unified Protestant denominations. All sorts of insurgent groups were present, worshipping together, with a collective vision and missional purpose.[38]

Campmeetings openly defied ecclesiastical standards of time, space, authority, and liturgical form. Campmeetings moved beyond the once-radical field preaching of Wesley, shifting attention from conspicuous preaching performances to congregational participation. Supernatural manifestations and uncensored testimonials by persons with no respect to age, gender, or race were normative. Public sharing of private ecstasy, overt physical display and emotional release, loud and spontaneous response to preaching, and the use of folk music were included among Methodist innovations.[39]

African Americans, both freedmen and slaves, were attracted to the informal and spontaneous nature of the Methodist gatherings. They participated as equals alongside White people. The message of personal holiness cut across racial, social, and economic lines, and Black leaders were encouraged to become preachers.[40] Harry Hosier, whom we will explore in depth later, was one who responded to the call.

Another encouraging development from revival throughout these turbulent times was how indigenous peoples found a place in the movement. In 1833, Turtle Fields became the first ordained indigenous Methodist Episcopal Church minister, and indigenous leaders have been serving as Methodist ministers ever since.

In essence, these innovations were reaching new people, breaking stereotypes, upturning social conventions, and creating new spaces and ways to worship. Or as we say in Fresh Expressions Florida, new people, new places, new ways. Our brief review of early nineteenth-century agrarian church history in the United States reminds us that these innovations were propagated by rural churches in rural places.

Our intent with this book is to show how this layer of soil needs a fresh ploughing to further the mission of the twenty-first-century church.

And yet, we want to be careful not to idealize the nineteenth-century expansion or suggest some romantic era of Christianity to which we need to return. Every movement has its issues because movements are made up of people and human beings are flawed.

Tragically, other layers of soil soaked in blood would follow. During the antebellum era (the period between the War of 1812 and before the Civil War of 1861 to 1865), men, women, and children became rifle-wielding Christian warriors, licensed to kill "Indian hostiles." While Methodists were among the first to license and ordain women, natives, and persons of color, they backpedaled on a firm commitment to abolish slavery. The Civil War saw Methodists on both sides killing each other in the name of God's righteous cause. Examining the soil requires attention to what ought to be utilized and what ought to be learned from. While the trajectory of this narrative is beautiful, it is not pure.

Ploughing the Soil

There's truth in what the Preacher[41] said about the cycle of history: "Whatever has happened—that's what will happen again; whatever has occurred—that's what will occur again. There's nothing new under the sun" (Ecclesiastes 1:9).

While we can't idealize the past, we can learn from these movements. Are there principles, processes, and frameworks from our origins on the land that might help rural congregations thrive today? We suggest that fresh energy for our missionary task in the current atmosphere of secularization and the overall declining vitality of Christianity can be found deep in the soils of our history. As we will discuss later, roots and growth are inextricably linked.

The distinct contours of rural consciousness have a long history. While congregations have in large part lost their role as a mediating institution, our churches played a fundamental role in shaping the rural mind-set that exists today.

The "spiritual but not religious" spirit that spreads through the United States in the twenty-first century is nothing new. This impulse to react against the establishment was pioneered by insurgent Christian movements. We can work with these impulses to catalyze positive kingdom impact in rural communities across the United States.

One universal challenge in every congregation, in every time and space, is *evangelization*. We define evangelizing in the sense of holistic processes by which people come to follow Jesus as Lord and are initiated into God's kingdom.

The challenges of evangelizing a new land are different than re-evangelizing a post-Christendom land. However, there are some particulars that have universal application.

We have seen rural congregations that recovered an insurgent and radically democratized nature, now thriving in this new space. We can learn from circuit riders, contextual expressions of faith, and utilizing emerging forms of communication.

The seeds of a church's renewal are hidden in the soils of the local congregations.

No outsider, guru, or denominational consultant can come and fix our problems for us. We must plough our own fields. The adaptive challenge is ours to navigate. Contextualizing the gospel and forming new Christian communities with people outside the church will look different in every rural place.

We suggest that the Fresh Expressions movement has many points of contact with the insurgent forms of Christianity that shaped the rural landscape. A fresh expression is a form of church for our changing culture, established primarily for the benefit of those who are not yet part of any church.[42]

We will show that for the rural church, "fresh expressions" are not all that fresh. They bloom from the soil in which the roots of rural congregations have grown.

Fresh Expressions language can help rural congregations rediscover their apostolic roots. It gives "expression" and process for the kind of radical democratization that was once the hallmark of early rural ministry. It breaks down the clergy/laity hierarchy, and it releases a priesthood of all believers. It creates space for people of different racial, political, and cultural differences to form true community, or circles that heal. It helps reaffirm a commitment to place, but reimagines a parish as an ecosystem that requires mobilization and shared leadership.

We, too, can utilize emerging technology and communication channels to connect people and mobilize movements. We can abandon big-box, church-growth strategies and rurally irrelevant vitality metrics, to rediscover what is healthy for us. We can stop forms of toxic charity. We can reconsider ministry "*for* the poor," as ministry *of*, *by*, and *with* the poor.

We find fresh hope when we understand that God always starts in the wilderness with marginalized people on the edge. We can break free from the individualistic idea of evangelism as saving souls for heaven when we die, and discover a place economy and how to practice daily living in God's realm. On a sick planet, this enables the rural church to play a vital role in creation care.

We are both practitioners of rural ministry, as are those whose stories we have collected in this book. We've seen the seeds of these ideas take root and lead to kingdom fruitfulness. We hope you will get together a team to work through this resource together. Get ready for a wild ride!

We are calling for a barnstorm in the backcountry. This book is a manifesto for rural leaders who want to create new networks that transform the landscape of communities across the United States. We are calling for rural congregations to draw resources from the center to the circumference.

Field Manual

Here's how this book works:

We envision this book as a field manual for teams to work through together.

Field Exercises: Following each chapter these exercises are designed to help your team roll up your sleeves and get some dirt beneath your fingernails as you seek to apply the principles to your own unique context.

Field Stories: Following the exercises you'll find interviews with practitioners and thought leaders of rural ministry. This book is a collaborative work; each story will help your team dream forth new possibilities.

The State of Rural Places

Welcome to the Wilderness

The LORD said to Abram, "Leave your land,
your family, and your father's household
for the land that I will show you." (Genesis 12:1)

I (Tyler) live in a place best described as nowhere. Metamora, Ohio: population 645. The miniscule village of Metamora is better known as a part of the Evergreen Local School District; a composition of what was once six small villages and several townships whose only contemporary function is to serve as address indicators, which reflects rural consolidation during the late twentieth and early twenty-first centuries.

As it goes with most rural villages, Metamora is a place of decline. The once-thriving and sufficient economies that supported the towns and tributary landscapes—partly for their usefulness as travel connections in the days of railroads and horses—has become a vacant tribute to a stagnant past. There's more corn than people, buildings, and imagination combined. The intergenerational pattern of heirs is a rarity, and the abandoned homes sit waiting for a return that only tends to occur for funerals. Food access is minimal, with a small handful of casual diners, a pizza parlor, and the occasional roadside produce stand. The closest grocery store is approximately twenty minutes away. There is, however, a meat market—St. Mary's Meats—which reveals interest to reclaim once known local food (which many of those still alive fondly remember). What was a rural food cooperative has survived the cultural shift of rural decline and still operates next to a cemetery with a sign that reads, "Fresh Cut Meats."

Our rural community passes all the perceived distinctions of rural life: mostly white- and blue-collar;[1] a few small industries with lots of agriculture; and perceived as backwards, underdeveloped, provincial, and primitive. At best, our greatest usefulness is seen as a recreational retreat or retirement to the countryside. At worst, we are a business opportunity, a place to be developed by the kind souls who intervene on our behalf because of our land, workforce, and lighter taxes. They also kindly brought jobs, metropolitan services, and access to products once considered luxurious. With the increase in transportation capability, rural areas became a place to live by happenstance or unfortunate inheritance. Why live here when you can access the cultural goods of life more easily in the suburbs, or be surrounded by the epicenter of civilized disconnection and ease of the city? Rural places are just worse versions of societal demand with less cellular coverage, slower internet, and quaint yet boring driving distances.

This has been the story of rural places.

Economically, rural communities are a microcosmic version of periphery economies—an export of raw materials. Local influence has been replaced by absentee control or utter vacancy. When 80 percent of the working population commutes twenty minutes or more for their occupation, it leaves quite the unstimulated mark on local vitality. Between the desire for transience and the loss of economic power, alongside the willingness to placate industrialization in a globalized world, rural communities are left with fragile populations.

We've also become primarily consumers, pouring our capital into places not our own. The hallmarks of rural life—connection to neighbors, connection to the land, and connection to forthcoming generations—has been replaced. Mutual responsibility is no longer necessary. Unfortunately, it appears that we've made a deal, and in becoming dependent on people we do not know and who do not care about us, we've become useless to each other. The supposedly civilized affluence and influence has nonchalantly separated us from the very source of our life that once made rural areas subsistent and connected. Rural people are not only irrelevant but also archaic and futile. Urban folk and metropolitan ideals are what really matter, and we must be avoided or corrected, possibly even colonized.

What does the death of a community cost? What is the result of the displacement of 24 million farmers? What happens when people leave or detach from a community? Rural dislocation and rural decline are unfortunate dance partners, turning rural places into a desolate wilderness.

Rural communities are now the places called nowhere made up of people called no one.

I (Michael) live in a place best described as forgotten. I live in the wild. Wildwood, Florida: population 7,276. In 2022, Wildwood is considered a city, but that label is misleading. A recent annexation of property makes Wildwood city limits extend more than forty square miles, one of Florida's largest in terms of geography. Much of that land is undeveloped. However, times are changing in Wildwood; it is a liminal space, in a time of transition.

According to legend, in 1877, a work crew from nearby Ocala was putting in a telegraph line heading south. The central office sent out a message to the surveyor and crew leader, "Where are you?" He responded, "I don't know, except in the wild woods." Hence, the little outpost became known as the "Wildwood" ever since.

The prevailing narrative tells of a twenty-five-year-old entrepreneur named I. E. Barwick who traveled down from Georgia to set up a lumber operation. Wanton S. Webb published a history of Florida in 1885, in which he describes Wildwood as being settled in 1877 by I. E. Barwick.[2] Barwick and a small company of pioneers built a few stores, homes, and a town square. These early settlers engaged in agricultural pursuits, including growing and selling cotton.

Among these first settlements was an 1881 Methodist Episcopal South church plant, which originally began meeting in the sanctuary of the newly constructed Presbyterian church. Reverend W. C. Collins, the founding planter, had the church constituted as a formal congregation in 1882. Our foundations sadly originated in a denomination that emerged from the 1844 schism over slavery in the Methodist Episcopal Church. In 1939, Methodist Episcopal South congregations were reunited with the northern congregations and in 1968 became connected to the newly formed United Methodist Church. Today, Wildwood United Methodist Church is one of those congregations.

Of course, the "wild wood" was not as wild as the white-washed histories would have us believe. The history books largely fail to note the indigenous tribes that lived with this land and called it home for over 12,000 years, or one of the oldest historic Black communities in Florida—Royal—founded here in 1865. Just five short miles from Wildwood UMC, this community of freed slaves settled here under Special Field Order 15, which granted the distribution of forty-acre lots and a surplus army mule. Some of the descendants of this community, whom you will meet later, trace their blood lines back to African royalty. Hence, for the Black community the name remains today, Royal.

Wildwood was once known as "the Crossroads of Florida." Geographically it's a central location for transportation. The economic engine of Wildwood became the railroad in the early 1800s and a community of local restaurants, shops, and an inn built up around the railroad station. In the 1960s, with the decline of the railroad industry and the relocation of the central station, the economy collapsed. Most of the families worked directly for the railroad or mined the economic opportunities it created. For decades the population lived in a state of economic desperation. Today, Wildwood is a train station graveyard, a fitting metaphor for the town itself.

However, while the train industry was failing during the 1960s, just a dozen miles to the northeast of Wildwood, a Michigan businessman named Harold Schwartz and his partner, Al Tarrson, obtained huge tracts of undeveloped land for bargain prices. They began selling these land tracts via mail. That is, they did until a 1968 federal law banned sales of real estate by mail order, leaving them with huge swaths of undeveloped land. So they opened a mobile home park for retirees, which would ultimately grow and expand into The Villages, Florida.

Today, The Villages, a master-planned age-restricted retirement community, is a sprawling city. Population 139,822. Between 2010 and 2020, The Villages was the fastest growing metropolitan area in the United States, growing 39 percent, from 93,000 to 130,000. It covers an area of approximately thirty-two square miles, an area larger than Manhattan, and is expanding mostly to the south of the current community. It has engulfed portions of Lake, Marion, and Sumter counties, including a little declining railroad town called Wildwood, Florida.

So describing Wildwood as a city with 7,200 residents is inaccurate. Four hundred acres of The Villages complex are now within the city limits of Wildwood, including two residential communities and the newest town square. The developers see more opportunities on the horizon, projecting that the population could run as high as 60,000 people by 2035. And yet, Wildwood and The Villages, while sharing the same zip code, are two very different contexts. The width of a wall separates the two communities, but they are worlds apart.

Co-pastor Jill Beck arrived with me in Wildwood twelve years ago. We moved into a parsonage with rolling fields and cows grazing in our back yard. The railroad graveyard was just a couple-blocks walk down the peaceful roads. Now our backyard has been annexed as The Villages property, and the wall replaced the open fields. The wall is designed to keep us Wildwood residents out. Just on the other side of the wall is a town square, dozens of restaurants, a high-end movie theater, and multiple supermarkets. We have watched a city spring up and surround our little rural space, but the "wild woods" itself has retained its rural identity.

Today, many people know Wildwood as the truck stop, or a place they pass through to get to Walt Disney World to the south or The Villages on the East. Villagers refer to the historically Black west side of Wildwood as the dangerous place you don't go at night. It's a forgotten space. A little pocket of wild you cross through accidentally to get where you're going. As the cycles of history show, new stories are written over previous ones by those who control the twin ogres of colonialism and capitalism. Entire peoples get buried under the layers, forgotten.

What hope is there for the forgotten ones? Those who chose to live and die in the wild of the rural? Those who hear change knocking at their back door but refuse to answer? How can a little dwindling congregation, a lost tribe of wild ones with a sketchy past, reimagine itself, reorganize, and guide the larger community to a better future?

The Bible has something to say about these questions.

The God of the Wilderness

The story of Abraham in Genesis is preceded by a subtle yet necessary detail, which might be overlooked. This detail establishes a setting for Abraham's covenant with God: "Terah took his son Abram, his grandson Lot (son of Haran), and his son Abram's wife, Sarai his daughter-in-law. They left Ur of the Chaldeans for the land of Canaan, and arriving at Haran, they settled there" (Genesis 11:31).

A spiraling progression of generational conflict persists in Genesis. From brothers killing brothers over game hunting and agricultural disputes (4:1-16) to a proliferating human society becoming so violent that God restarts creation (6–9) and the Babel tower that pursues immortality by creating a tower that reaches to the skies, which would be the ultimate feat of technological progress and sociological centralization in the civilized world. Genesis remains suspicious of such development.

Abram—whose name will be changed by covenant to Abraham—begins his journey in Ur; a geographical location that is in some textbooks recalled as the birthplace of civilization. Ur was the first dominant city in ancient Mesopotamia, which would be home to the Sumerians. (By the sixth century BCE, this area would be dominated by Babylon, the epicenter of empire, progress, and civilizing forces of culture.)

The origin story of Israel begins with leaving such a place (to which it will return in exile).

The land of Canaan would have seemed like the opposite of Ur. In most respects, it was a place of nomadic wandering and social outcasts. Abram leaves the epicenter of his known world to go to the middle of nowhere. Abram's travels would have taken him and his family from the hub of civilization through progressively smaller cities and eventually to the wilderness. Imagine leaving New York City and journeying through Philadelphia, then Pittsburgh, with brief stops in Cleveland and Chicago, and ending up in the middle of a cornfield in Iowa. That's analogous to what Abram is doing at the end Genesis 11.

In some biblical stories, when God is going to intervene, God begins in the wilderness. Moses leaves the empire of Egypt to meet God at Sinai; Elijah retreats to a remote overlook to hear the still, small voice; Isaiah declares that Israel's future will begin in a desolate landscape; Paul leaves the Damascus road and first removes himself to the nothingness of Arabia; and Jesus, of course, is from the hick town of Nazareth, with his ministry initiated in the wilderness.

Hear this good news: the story of God often begins in the wilderness.

The places called nowhere and the people called no one are the setting for God's work in the world.

There's something about rural places, especially considering their decline, that parallels wilderness theology, and rural places may just be the desolate places where God's work is primed to unfold. They are important, if not essential.

The Importance of Rural Places

Why would God so frequently be encountered in the wilderness experience? In terms of social and economic forces, is there anything about desolate landscapes and declining rural communities that might further their importance?

Consider the 2016 election. Widely considered to be an extraordinary departure from the expectations of typical presidential politics, the vote hinged on an overlooked factor—the rural population. Tex Sample pulls together research to disprove the thesis that rural and working-class America rejected a woman and preferred Donald Trump for the office.[3] However, the 2016 election undoubtably brought more rural people to the polls than ever before, and the rural vote played an important role in the outcome. An important voter cohort was ignored by some and manipulated by others.

Metamora, Ohio, or Wildwood, Florida, compared to Los Angeles or New York City, are nothing. However, 60 million people in thousands of small towns and rural counties covering 97 percent of the nation's land mass is a bit more significant. Seventy-six percent of incorporated places are home to fewer than 5,000 people, and 42 percent have fewer than 500 people. That's 19,500 official communities that are rural, and thousands more that don't register in the census bureau's categories.[4] Do these places matter? Further, are they impactful? Should they be considered in the dialogue about solving the world's problems and charting the world's future. Should they have a voice?

The 2016 election showed that a voice is present. But what about when those people take responsibility for almost every acre of land? What if that land is necessary to produce food for the other 270 million people? If an economy is affected most by where the economy originates and is produced, shouldn't we want to nurture the thriving of such places? And what if those people have developed a particular history and skills over time to be able to do so? Even if technology and science and our abstract hopes for the future make us believe such land and skills are not necessary, we can't help but wonder if the diverse heritage, memories, and abilities are still worth considering in our modern towers of Babel. We suppose it depends on the standards and values prioritized in the human experience. Among the population groups, the land use, the histories, and the skills, it appears that rural places are worth considering.

These places with so much perceived cultural deficit may be in possession of something quite useful. Rural communities carry the stigma of being primitive, but it may be because they give credence to something our culture has long forgotten: each other.

We resist falling into the two polarizing myths about rural communities: (1) that they are communitarian, deeply moral, agrarian paradises or (2) that they are in decay and failing. We will demonstrate that rural communities are much more diverse and complicated than that.

True, rural communities may be unfortunate in thousands of ways, but they may have the one thing our world needs: a place to belong.

When one's life is enmeshed in the lives and the world around it, a certain dependence unfolds in respect to the source of one's life. Hence, the wilderness may not just be a theologically abstract theme but a sociological and historical necessity. God's propensity toward the wilderness doesn't seem random, because there's something about the wilderness that makes a better world possible.

Declining rural places may, therefore, deserve our attention and respect. They ought to garner the kind of credibility that comes with their potential power and capability.

Allen Stanton notes, "While urban communities can be easily identified, rural communities exist as a spectrum. Definitions of rural capture snapshots rather than painting a whole portrait, in large part because the whole portrait is nearly impossible to capture."[5] Many kinds of communities fall under the umbrella of the title *rural*. As you might observe in our personal stories, and the field stories that follow each chapter, each of us live and serve in the rural, but our contexts are incredibly unique.

Every context is similar to a *tel*, a Hebrew or Arabic term for "mound." This is a topographical feature, consisting of the accumulated and stratified debris of a succession of consecutive settlements built up on the same site. Rural communities have layers of stories, the sediment of generations of people who lived with the land. Some caused harm, others cultivated healing, and most did a bit of both. In many contexts, the soils are stained with blood.

Just as archeologists are skilled at excavating a *tel*, rural church leaders need to excavate the stories of their place. We must dig into, examine, and turn over the sediment of those stories. Cultivating fresh expressions in the rural place requires this contextual excavation.

Increasingly, rural places are becoming desolate landscapes. Forgotten people in forgotten places. Is there, then, an organization, movement, or body that exists to catalyze this potential and see to the future of the landscapes and communities of which they are in?

There is.

It's called the local church.

A healthy rural church could be that which changes everything and, if the work of God typically begins in the wilderness, rural places are poised to channel the renewal of the church.

Maybe God is again beckoning to leave Ur and begin building a good world from the apparent emptiness. Our purpose is to explore how we might do so. Our hope is that, if we are obedient to the divine precedent, the whole world will never be the same.

Let's reimagine the church in the wild.

CHAPTER 1

The Hope of the Rural Church

On Being Thornbushes

The LORD's messenger appeared to him in a flame
of fire in the middle of a bush.
Moses saw that the bush was in flames,
but it didn't burn up. (Exodus 3:2)

Have you ever considered what type of burning bush Moses encountered when God showed up? The invasive species called "burning bush" (*euonymus alatus*) takes its colloquial name from the story.

Exodus 3 tells us the bush was aflame though not consumed when Moses spotted it in the wilderness. Putting plant taxonomy aside, is there any value in considering the binomial nomenclature of the burning shrub in the wilderness? Ancient rabbinic commentaries on the book of Exodus believed the curious endeavor was worth pursuing. The rural church may want to follow the lead of such an uncanny cue.

I (Michael) am a cross-cultural missionary to the rural context. I grew up in the city of Ocala, Florida: population 63,591. I was sent as a supply pastor to my first congregation, Lochloosa, Florida: population 47. The church sits back in the woods off a winding dirt road. No post office. No stop lights. No gas station. No Walmart.

Our guest worship team played harps, banjos, a kick drum, and an unfamiliar instrument called an autoharp (a string instrument belonging to the zither family). People worshipped barefoot. We took off our shoes and slid them under the pews because that's what the Holy God who shows up in the flames of a burning bush tells us to do.

On a good Sunday at Lochloosa, we worshipped around twelve people, and every person was related to one of two families, whose ancestors settled here and planted the church in the late 1800s. How do you "grow" a congregation like this using the standard institutional metrics of "success"? You know, average worship attendance, professions of faith, apportionments paid, and an expense versus giving comparison, or in short, "nickels and noses." With a place holding a population of forty-seven, there wasn't much to work with.

It was helpful that our blended family of eight kids doubled the congregation on the first Sunday. But we learned very quickly that those metrics would not fit what vitality would look like for us.

We ate frequently at the local diner in Hawthorne seven miles up the road, since it was the only place to eat nearby. One day it dawned on us, as we were conversing with the servers whom we knew on a first-name basis, and we asked, "What would church look like for you?" They were the persons who "share God's peace" with us (Luke 10:6). The ones Jesus tells us to find, connect with, and share life at the table in the places to which we are sent. They couldn't attend church on Sundays because they were busy serving church people meals. So we co-created a church together with them, over barbecue-laden tables.

In the span of one year, our little congregation of twelve did grow by all institutional growth metrics, but the vitality wasn't captured on any report. It was in the relationships. The exchange of stories. The willingness to risk leaving the confines of church as we know it, to create something fresh and incarnational together. Those were lessons we took to our next appointment on the rural circuit, Wildwood, Florida.

Previously I described the "wild ones" and their forgotten stories. Let's excavate a little deeper.

What those first White "settlers" called the "wild woods" was called simply "home" by others. Seminole Indians, as well as Miccosukees and other tribes, have had ancestors peacefully existing upon these lands for at least 12,000 years. Following the War of 1812 between the United States and Britain, American slave owners came to Florida in search of runaway African slaves and "Indians" who had been trading weapons and supporting the British. The First Seminole War occurred from 1817 to 1818, when the United States Army invaded Spanish Florida and fought against the Seminole and their Black allies.

The Seminole struggle over their native land included many skirmishes and several major battles. In 1829, Andrew Jackson became President of the United States. Congress passed his Indian Removal Act into law in 1830. The act legitimated the forced movement of all Indians to land west of the Mississippi River.

A Seminole warrior named Chief Osceola led his tribe in a series of surprise attacks against the Americans throughout Wildwood and the larger area of Sumter County. The first major battle became known as the Dade Massacre. Major Dade was leading a combined army from Fort Brooke (Tampa) and Fort King (Ocala). Osceola's warriors attacked and killed over a hundred soldiers throughout the "wild woods." Eventually, Osceola was captured and died in prison in 1838. The handful of Seminole that were still in Florida decided to withdraw into the Everglades rather than surrender. Some still reside there to this day. Sadly, the indigenous population of the Florida peninsula, estimated at 200,000 in 1500, is less than 3,000 today.

Another aspect of this wild space, which goes largely unmentioned in the history of the White settlers, is the Black community of Royal. Just across Gator Pond from Wildwood UMC, is one of Florida's oldest Black communities. Founded in 1865, over a decade before the first surveyor and crew came trampling through the "wild woods," the community of Royal existed peacefully with the land. The White invaders renamed it Picketsville, after the white picket fences that marked the homes inhabiting these no-more-than-forty-acre homesteads, granted under Special Field Order 15.

Royal was settled by former slaves from the Old Green Plantation located on the Withlacoochee River. After the Civil War, the residents quietly changed its name back to "Royal," which was documented as early as 1880. The families of Royal trace their ancestry back to African kings, queens, princes, and princesses. My friend and co-collaborator in good trouble, Beverly Steele, is one of those original families of royal descent. Steele grew up in Royal during segregation, which she witnessed coming to an end in the 1970s. She has preserved this largely forgotten history so future generations of all races would always know that some of the first Blacks in this place came from African royalty.

The legacy of colonialism, slavery, racism, and segregation is preserved in the Wildwood community today. Essentially, there is a railroad track down the middle of the town, with predominantly White folk living on one side and Black folk living under the influences of systemic racism on the other. Lynchings, Ku Klux Klan activity, and signs reading "no niggers after dark" are part of this community's history. Sadly, the churches, including the one I serve as pastor, have been complicit in preserving the racism and inequality.

When the first train arrived on June 1, 1882, the economy began to boom. The Tropical Florida Railroad extended a line south from Ocala. The train was pulled by a wood-burning engine called "The Cabbage Head." Florida's railroad network grew rapidly. By 1880 it boasted over 500 miles of track. During the industry's heyday, Florida was home to six major railroads, only one of which is still operational today. The current station was built in 1947 by the Seaboard Air Line Railroad. The Silver Meteor and the Silver Star trains split at Wildwood, with one section continuing to Miami, Florida, and the other serving St. Petersburg and Sarasota–Venice on Florida's west coast. For many decades, the majority of residents were employed by the railroad in some capacity.

In the late 1960s, the railroad industry began to disappear. What was once a thriving hub of transportation activity became a graveyard for trains no longer in use. Local shops and restaurants built up around the railroad station were forced to close. Today, the station operates as a CSX maintenance yard and by Amtrak's Thruway Motorcoach bus service between Jacksonville and Lakeland. The actual station building remains, but the platform was demolished.

During that same period, amidst the economic decline, Schwartz and Tarrson were envisioning opportunity. When the partners got stuck with huge portions of Florida land, in the early 1970s, they began development of a mobile home park, Orange Blossom Gardens. Schwartz then bought out Tarrson's interest and brought his son, H. Gary Morse, on board in 1983.

They began to buy large tracts of land in nearby Sumter and Marion counties for future expansion of a retirement community, modeled after other successful retirement communities nearby. By the early 1990s, they had more than 8,000 residents, three golf courses, a Winn-Dixie supermarket, four restaurants, and nightly dances held in a tent. In 1992, Morse officially named the development The Villages.

Mayor Wolf, who has served as mayor of Wildwood for over twenty-six years sees hope for Wildwood in a tourist attraction, where people come to visit the quaint little shops on the town square. It's now a relic of a past age, like a time capsule, where people can come visit a little piece of history, then retreat back into the affluence of their preplanned homes spaced seven feet apart in rows that stretch for miles. The Village's residents call this the "bubble." Their neighborhoods look eerily like those in the movie The Truman Show,[1] with preproduced, perfectly manicured sets, where people enjoy an endless list of retirement activities. Visiting the little failed railroad town helps them recover a connection to history and, in my opinion, reality.

While some Wildwood residents have embraced this reality, many have not, including some who called Wildwood UMC their home. The Villages was a threat, an empire of consumerism, spreading their way, swallowing up their land and their cows, replacing them with rows of preplanned houses. The Villages "bubble" is a self-contained ecosystem. They also built their own churches—big ones. The thousands of retirees moving in, and aging out, need a congregation to call home until they die. By and large the churches embrace the consumeristic culture of the larger community. You can come to church in your golf cart and finish with plenty of time to play a few holes on any of the 50 golf courses and 2,500 clubs and activities.

Most people fail to see the disintegration of the Wildwood schools. The Villages has their own charter schools, from pre-K to high school, with new state-of-the art facilities and high educational standards for their teachers. One of the perks for working-class families to move to the area and work in The Villages is to access a superior education for their children. Meanwhile, the Wildwood high school and middle school had to be combined into one school, and simply cannot compete with The Villages Charter School.

On the White side of the tracks, the old Wildwood families who stayed are dying off or being bought out; but on the west side the Black community remains largely unchanged. They can peer across the tracks and see a wall, on the other side of which is affluence, comfort, and the culmination of White privilege. The Villages community is 98.8 percent White and boasts about the lowest crime rate in Florida. For the Black community of Wildwood, there have been few opportunities knocking at their door. Drug dealing, service industry, and low-paying construction jobs seem to be the options. The neighborhood is plagued by gun violence, with multiple murders making headlines every year.

Many people move into Wildwood to get jobs in The Villages' service industry, but this creates a transient population, changing frequently. One little building in the town center has not changed with it—a little congregation known affectionately today as the "wild ones" of Wildwood UMC.

The Black community and Wildwood in general have identified like a thornbush at the edge of prosperity. But what if our lost tribe outside the wall is actually at the center of God's activity? What if, as the oldest institution in the community, we are one of the few permanent stakeholders? What if there in the wild we possess precious resources, ablaze with God's glory, but not burned up?

The Lost Tribe

The church just ain't what it used to be. Not a year goes by without a consultant or pollster announcing what most of us already know: that the church in the Western world is in decline, with dwindling congregations and a burgeoning group called the "nones." The once-feared secularization of post-Christian culture is assumably here.

There are still 250 to 300 hundred thousand churches in the United States (over 80 percent considered small), and something feels amiss. What was a subversive, revolutionary tribe of people moving through the world, so as to restore it, has become more and more obsolete, often incompetent. Occasionally, this is manifested by abandoned church buildings pocketed in neighborhoods or on country roads. Meanwhile, the fad of taking old, nostalgic churches and converting them to restaurants or homes is increasingly normal. How long before there are more churches-turned-breweries than churches themselves?

What has gone amiss, however, may not require much speculation. The decline of the church is the responsibility of the church. Millions of people, it seems, look elsewhere for hope. Is this because the subversive tribe has lost its identity? Have we, in turn, become part of the problem that our world seeks to heal?

When considering rural churches and their communities, the decline and demise occur in parallel. How we respond to our tenuous situation involves more than keeping our churches from becoming museums; our response has implications for the future of the places we inhabit. But it will involve fulfilling the sacred identity of this lost tribe called the church.

Reimagining the Church in the Wild

Local churches—especially in rural communities—typically were central to the life of the places they inhabit, and not primarily through sermons during Sunday morning church services. In the early church, the primacy of local communities was so normative that it led to the first ecumenical councils. Early Christianity had to get everyone together to find common bonds, because local communities were so heavily reflective of their unique place. Yes, there were political agendas involved in these ecumenical endeavors, but the local vitality led to contextual diversity because the church's primary emphasis was to be rooted in the places they met.

Despite politicking and the tragedies of church power struggles, the local significance survived. This cue came from early Judaism. Just as the Apostle Paul could find a place of solace in any community at the local synagogue, so too have travelers been able to venture into a community and find a local church, often acting as the hub of the town. At their best, local churches offered a place to gather with an intention to serve their larger community—a body that exists for the good of the larger body. This decision or instinct to make local manifestations the heart of a global movement gave the movement immense propensity. It also preserves the key for our lost movement to recover its essence.

Consider the enlivening discussion about community—a trendy monolith of a concept, but also the core necessity to human survival and flourishing. There are four primary ingredients necessary to establish community:

- Shared history: consistently developing experience over time.

- Shared imagination: a common direction or vision that gives a bond, purpose, and identity to the group.

- Proximity: the actual, physical presence of people.

- Permanence: a committed rootedness and promised connection for the indefinite continuation of the group's identity.

Each church has a foundational mechanism that intentionally functions to mix these ingredients. Well-conceived churches are primed with a particular vision (shared imagination), they occupy an intergenerational longevity that transcends any one generation (permanence), they are able to reflect a place's heritage and memory by continuing that longevity in respect to the present (shared history), and their function is to be physically connected to their neighbors and context (proximity). Of the many sociological patterns driving human history, the church appears to be one of the most prolific mediums of community.

We, as Christians, have a teleological vision of universal flourishing, but that vision is enacted by millions of people in thousands of unique places through meaningful adaptation. The kingdom of God can be transposed into infinite contexts because of the intentional presence and care of local churches. Forming human beings, nurturing relationships, supporting communal and social organizations, creating opportunities for belonging among neighbors, and impacting a place's economic life—this happens best by meaningfully adapting the vision of the kingdom of God in the small places where we are. We can look at our geographical areas and ask, "What would it look like if God's economy were in charge here?" And then we can mobilize practical action to bring that vision into immediate reality. The nature of the people of God is to imagine and realize such a dream. The presence of real people in those real locations provides the opportunity to do so.

The issues inhibiting the present-day churches are not the result of a lack of structure or capability or purity. We do not need to change "the

Church." Nor do we need to invent new ideas. We simply need to reclaim our essence, establishing local community, a mission that is still compelling and certainly available.

The invitation to declining churches in declining places is to reimagine each church by reimagining the places in which we reside. In light of rural desolation, yet in hope of rural capability, this hope may be best realized by churches in the wilderness. Even with the lingering gloom, there is much hope to be found in rural churches that embrace this purpose.

Healing the Garden

The prophet Jeremiah sent word to the exiles in Babylon for how they ought to embrace their bleak situation: "Promote the welfare of the city where I have sent you into exile. Pray to the LORD for it, because your future depends on its welfare" (Jeremiah 29:7).

How will the exiles endure? What is their directive in a world that has been destroyed? See to the welfare—the shalom—of the places where they are.[2] Hence, the ancient rabbis of early Judaism, when pondering the nature of the burning bush in Exodus 3, earnestly declared that it was, of course, a thornbush. When the divine presence appeared to founder Moses to unleash Israel's covenant throughout the world, it came through an image of the pristine garden of Genesis. As the rabbinic commentary goes, the garden of creation was surrounded by thornbushes as a hedge of protection; a source of preservation to foster the vitality of God's garden. The symbol of the bush theophany implies that Israel, too, is meant to be a thornbush for the world—a hedge that protects, preserves, and contributes to the sustainability of all creation.

Each church planted is the continuation of this covenantal vision for God's garden, or in New Testament imagery, God's kingdom. Each body of Christ exists for the good of a larger body of neighbors in their geographic place. The common good is measured by the health, vitality, and future of their community. Each church is meant to be a thornbush for the place it inhabits. Therefore for so many centuries, churches were the hubs of their communities. The local church has the proven propensity to form, nurture, support, and unleash the kingdom of God by fostering the health of a place and seeking its shalom. When that mission becomes contagious, our hope for the future fof the world becomes palpable.

Though the world has looked elsewhere, people are still looking for something. Fortunately, our tradition is built to offer that something. But how does this happen, especially in rural churches?

The Church of Rock Bottom

Now for the difficult news.

Humans not only tend to dislike change but also are biologically and socially predisposed to resisting it. Accepting the wilderness journey is a weight we probably wouldn't wish for, let alone choose. Fortunately, it no longer appears that we have a choice.

The church that I (Tyler) currently lead faced this reality explicitly. I came to Metamora, Ohio, out of naiveté and reluctance. I was poor, unemployed, and desperately searching for stability after moving from California. Receiving a call to a pastoral appointment offered reprieve. The situation was a bit disconcerting. The appointment needed filling because the pastor at the church had died unexpectedly, and the church was on the brink of closing.

I decided to drive out to the church to see what I faced. Suburban development had slowly evolved into cornfields, a setting both unfamiliar and daunting. There was no development, barely any industry, and an almost imperceptible amount of human activity. There was also no church. A dilapidated building sat near the one street light in the village—a representation of how the whole village felt. The church hadn't been used in over a decade since it had been condemned because of black mold.

This wasn't just a rural church. It was a rural church in the middle of nowhere, with a dwindled congregation and every conceivable setback

I could imagine, suggesting that this church had hit rock bottom. It certainly felt like the wilderness. Needless to say, I requested a new appointment.

A few weeks went by, then a few months. I started to feel strangely at home, and the hope for an appointment change slowly faded. The stories and history of a unique place emerged from the rural stereotypes, like a palpable hope blossoming beneath the surface of death and decline. Even as an inexperienced twenty-four-year-old, I was welcomed into their fold. I realized, then, that the places called nowhere with people called no one were not only falsely described but actually contained a necessary ingredient for future possibility: complete desperation.

The best method for overcoming resistance is to have no other choice. In the recovery community, there is an acronym for G.O.D: Gift of Desperation. When we are at the end of our rope, in the powerlessness and unmanageability of our lives, there we find a fresh encounter with God.

In the book of Acts, there is a scene in which Jesus physically meets with his disciples for what will be the last time. For the body of Christ to continue the work, Jesus must leave it in their hands. The absence of their leader's body makes it possible for them to navigate the uncharted territory ahead. Jesus tells them that they will go to Jerusalem, Judea, Samaria, and the ends of the earth, and then Jesus ascends. They stand there staring at the sky (Acts 1:6-9). They are paralyzed by the enormousness of the possible. As the book of Acts commences, we find out they don't venture much past Jerusalem. They stay where they are until Acts 8.

The cause of their movement is poignantly noted: "At that time, the church in Jerusalem began to be subjected to vicious harassment. Everyone except the apostles was scattered throughout the regions of Judea and Samaria" (Acts 8:1). The church awakens when crushed. The desolate difficulty of daunting circumstances takes us where we might not naturally go ourselves.

The Farmhouse, this little, old rural Ohio church in the middle of nowhere on the brink of collapse, embodied the hope of the wild; it was the catalyzing force of emptiness and struggle that so often marks Israel's wandering, exile, and renewal. Complete desperation, when vulnerably embraced, leads to imagination. Desperation can take us where comfort cannot.

As I sat around a table with the few congregants who had trekked through the countryside, I asked what we were going to do. Their response? "We can either close our doors or start over. We might as well try something new."

When people ask me what they should do to revive their rural church, I coyly remark that they should put black mold in their buildings. The greatest catalyst for the church may be complete desperation. That's where God's work always begins.

Finding Hope in the Wilderness

Christian culture tends to carry a myopic view of the past—what we have known must be what has always been, and it must be what is right. It's frightening to let go. However, our nearsightedness might be holding us back. Like stagnant water, when the church becomes static, it becomes a malodorous, mosquito-infested swamp. If we are stuck in the swamp, we need a little prod into the wilderness, which means we need desperation to refuel imagination.

If we're honest, the situation of rural places is desperate. As we scan the dismal landscapes in our desolate wilderness, we take solace in our history. This mission is yet alive since that bush was aflame. Will we take on the identity of thornbushes in the places we inhabit? Will we structure our existence as a body for the good of the larger community? Will we be a signpost for God's kingdom by offering healing and hope, by cultivating transformation, and by supporting and guiding our communities toward God's dream for the world?

What else could the church be? Reimagining the church in rural areas might be the only thing we can do in our present circumstances; but it might also be the only thing we ought to do.

So how do we reimagine the church in our local communities?

We offer a map to be explored.

Field Exercise

Excavating Your Tel

With your team, excavate your Tel. Gather together to examine the "layers of story" that define your place. Use a tool such as https://missionin site.com or Google Analytics to collect the demographic data. Have someone on the team present key findings.

1. What are two or three defining stories for your community? What native groups inhabited this land? How did the area become incorporated? What families, organizations, businesses, industries, and government involvement were important for your place's development? What major events or changes have happened to bring the community to where it currently is?

2. What are two or three defining stories of your congregation? How did your church begin? Who was involved? Why did they start this particular church? What has changed in the last two hundred, one hundred, or even ten years?

3. What are the stories beneath the stories, or the truths that get swept under the rug? What moments of conflict or pain exist in your place's or church's history?

4. In what ways do you see your community as a "thornbush at the edge of progress"? Meaning, how is your faith subversive to the

overarching narratives? How is your church continuing the story of the place where you are?

5. In what ways are you experiencing "desperation"?

6. In what ways is this desperation a gift?

7. What do you imagine for your larger community? Perhaps prompt responses with, "If God were in charge here . . ."

Field Story

Mary Jackson, Pastor, Greater Bell in Brooker, Florida: population 390

I've been serving this primarily Black congregation in a rural community for eleven years. We have an average worship attendance of about eighty. There is a lot of farmland and very few businesses in the area. The church is located ten miles north of Gainesville, Florida, which has a population of 132,000.

Serving in a rural context is important to me because I grew up in a rural setting. I'm familiar with the customs and style of rural worship. I feel strongly that the rural church has the ability to reach out and make disciples of Jesus Christ for this changing world. However, it must be done in creative and strategic ways through leadership training.

Our church team had the opportunity to attend "Dinner Church" training. We read books, watched videos, and listened to dynamic speakers, and we shared this information with our leadership team. Even though we were entering uncharted territory in our town, we were willing to take a risk and step out on faith. From this training, we started a dinner church, not in our rural community of Brooker, but as a fresh expression in Gainesville.

We watched God move in this dinner church. We shared the stories of Jesus, we celebrated communion, baptisms were performed, and lives were changed. Keith was the first person baptized in the dinner church. Some of the people in the dinner church participated by singing and helping to lead worship. Lucille has a beautiful voice, and she would bless us by singing of her favorite song, "I Came to Tell You What Jesus Said."

Some would show up early and help us set up the community center and then stay afterward to help us put tables and chairs away. We were experiencing more people in worship at dinner church than in our Sunday morning worship service. Our dinner church expression is more diverse than our Sunday morning worship service. We are reaching more of God's people.

After the pandemic stopped us for some months, we resumed dinner church outside the community center building. Now we are inside with a limited capacity. God is still moving, and lives are changed each week as we see new faces coming to hear the good news shared over a delicious meal together.

CHAPTER 2

Rethinking the Parish

Barns and Bodies

You are the body of Christ and parts of each other. (1 Corinthians 12:27)

What would happen if your church closed?

It is a useful reflection exercise for churches contemplating their existence, but it is also a confrontational reminder of how we think about the parish.

Imagine, then, that your church closed its doors tomorrow. If this happened, who would care? Just you? Just the members of the church? What about the community? Would the local farmers and producers care? Would the working poor or food insecure care? Would the families on the brink of divorce care? What about those with addictions or depression? The question surfaces whether our church is just for the internal stakeholders or if the scope of church transcends our buildings.

If your church closed its doors, would it still be able to be the church in the place that it is?

In chapter 1, we described The Farmhouse, a small, rural church that actually experienced this question. Black mold forced the church to close its doors. No longer could they depend on the common components of the modern church experience. They couldn't be dependent on the use of a space, and, as a result, they had to consider what else the church could be. When you take away the normal constraints of accepted church models, you can begin to see opportunities previously hidden by assumptions. Have we limited our existence by presuming a church and a building are synonyms? Church buildings may be the biggest obstacle to a vibrant community of faith.

Body Building

Many Christians have witnessed the golden age of sanctuaries—an unprecedented era of church history spawning beautiful architecture and building-centric communities. It would be easy to assume that this is normal, that the words *church* and *church building* are synonyms. While church buildings have been a fixture of Western Christianity, they were mostly not present for the first 300 years of church history. It wasn't until Emperor Constantine began erecting grand structures after 327 CE throughout the Byzantine Empire that dedicated structures became a possibility for Christians. Constantine adapted the pagan practice of constructing magnificent temples to honor the gods. Still, many churches didn't have their own dedicated buildings until much later in history.

The early church shares numerous stories of the church gathering together—often to celebrate the Eucharist—but most of this happened in open, public spaces or on private property (i.e., someone's home). During the first several centuries of the church's existence, it would have been an anomaly for them to own property. Asking Christians from the first or second century where they went to church would probably result in puzzled looks. And "church shopping" would have been inconceivable. Churches were bonded communities with integral actions, rituals, and identities. When churches did have buildings, they functioned as a mobilization center, a communal space for gathering, or as monasteries. No one was trying to fill the pews, because quite literally there weren't any. The church was first and foremost a body.

The height of post-classical Europe brought the proliferation of buildings and sanctuaries—often intertwined with hosting the local political authority. The evolution of medieval architecture ensued, and the centralization of church authority continued the development of local church establishments. The history of church buildings—and the history of the church in general—is wrapped up in the cultural and sociological forces of feudalism, imperialism, colonialism, absolutism, enlightenment, and revolution. So, consider that what is currently normative was not always normal and has been confounded by layers of interest that had little to do with God's kingdom on earth.

In the pioneer expressions of Christianity that barnstormed through the backcountry of rural North America, we saw the church reassess its relationship with buildings and property. As we explore more fully in chapter 10, campmeetings were often held outside, and this created a sense of liminality in which the expected social hierarchy was challenged and reimagined. At the open-air campmeetings, people of different races and genders could sit together and actively participate.

As these movements began the process of institutionalization by trading out missional zeal for respectability, they reverted to racist tendencies. Howard Thurman notes in *Jesus and the Disinherited*, "Too often the price exacted by society for security and respectability is that the Christian movement in its formal expression must be on the side of the strong against the weak."[1] Respectability is usually the possession of those in power. For instance, as more and more Methodist church buildings were constructed and worship moved inside, it was considered inappropriate for Blacks and Whites to sit together.[2] This reversed the racial equality that was simmering in the campmeetings, leading to segregated worship and further discrimination toward persons of color. Property, a standard of denominational success and safety, actually reinforced inequality and hubris. We conflated the idea of a healthy church with beautiful, permanent structures dedicated to Christian worship. We treasure body building as if constructing a building will grow the body, even though building the body of Christ can take place without a building.

We have built buildings. They have not come or they have gone. Most modern Christians can grasp that the church is a body. However, beyond the acrobatic rhetoric, our tangible actions revert to the walls with a roof. Now what do we do with our empty or aging rural church buildings?

Guide and Gather

First, we seek consensus that the church is a body—a living, breathing web of relationships with a collective purpose. If we tire of the trite "body" metaphor, we can recall the rabbinic thornbushes that form an enflamed hedge around God's garden, God's realm.

God's people are invited into discipleship—to become thornbushes— to enact the good news. The presumed outcome is that the kingdom of God will be realized because the garden thrives more. This is the end goal of Jesus's good news.

Second, we talk about the buildings because, well, they are there. They might still be useful. Consider the church with black mold. Eventually they built a new building, though it is a barn. The primary reason was to help break the static perception about church buildings. Whatever one assumed a church building was supposed to look like, this was going to be different. Further, it allowed the church to give their building a collective use. In a rural community, barns are presumed architecture; barns reflect the geography and history of the landscapes. Therefore, the church without a building decided to create a space.

The "meeting tent" in the book of Leviticus functioned for wandering people who didn't need and couldn't possess a structure; they needed a space. They needed a collective place to be inspired for their return to other spaces.

Our rural spaces, therefore, are essential for guiding our communities. Rural communities often lack gathering space. In most rural places there are few third spaces—a realm between the private and the public. You can go to the school or grocery store and then you can go home, but there are few places to simply gather and be present to each other and with God. Many churches in rural areas isolate themselves as private spaces, over-against culture, and one needs membership credentials to have access.

Many rural congregations now take seriously the small group that gathers digitally. Can people connect, pray, learn, and worship together in an online environment? The pandemic forced many rural congregations to rethink their response to that question. Rural churches started Facebook groups, YouTube channels, and online campuses, and they worshipped in Zoom rooms, through phone conferencing technology, or on emerging virtual reality headsets. These gatherings are not disembodied. Our bodies are participating with our senses and our fingers. It's a different kind of third place. A different kind of built environment. A different kind of barn.

What does it look like for our churches to consider themselves as third spaces? How do we give more access and create both experiences and opportunities for our communities to have a space to gather and connect?

The church is a body, and it is also a barn, and it is also present with Christ on a screen.

So what are we guiding toward and gathering for? We cannot forget that the church already has a penultimate vision for our destination. The key word is *health*.

Healthy People, the Single Unit of Health

While we usually define health as physical or medical, health includes every system of life. The Christian tradition uses the term *salvation*. Our typical meaning for salvation may be too narrow; a wider definition draws from the Hebrew word *shalom*—well-being, universal flourishing. Salvation deals with the identity or destiny of a person, but it also is concerned with safety and food and economy and relationships.

Health is a good standard because it encompasses this fulness of salvation or shalom. As is often said in agrarian circles, the life of every part of a place passes through your life and affects it. From your holistic health as an individual being, to your relationships, to the social and economic health of a community and its social systems, to the ecological health of a geographic place where our lives are interdependent and determined. A threat to health anywhere is a threat to health everywhere.

Health is evident in our hearts, in our homes, and in our zip code when God's dream and God's realm are made real and full. Simply put, growing healthy in the biblical sense is about growing in love and being good stewards of each dimension. This leads to shalom.

The human condition is primarily in a state of recovery. Every human being is in recovery from selfish desires. Growth always begins from the starting point of brokenness. We are not our best selves unless we are becoming our best selves together. When we put our bodies together, whether it be in a barn, a field, a tattoo parlor, a sanctuary, or a Zoom room, there we have the potential for recovery.

Fresh Expressions Begin in the Fields

A movement of democratized forms of Christianity, inspired by John Wesley, spread across the rural frontier, meeting outdoors and empowering common people to play a part.

On April 2, 1739, at the urging of his friend George Whitefield, Wesley went to a field outside the city limits of Bristol, England. There he took up the "vile" practice of field preaching, which was scandalous to official church leaders. He recognized that many people were no longer coming "to church" and never would. He put his body in the field and formed church with people where they did life, and thousands of people began to gather in crowds.[3]

Wesley discovered the Spirit at work in the lives of people beyond the church walls. Because the world truly was his parish, Wesley's pulpit took many forms. In his open air preaching, church formed in parks, public and private gardens, churchyards, lofts, barrack-yards, barns, streets, theaters, private homes, front porches, city malls, general recreation grounds, miners' camps, prisons, paved stairs, gateways, mansions, open squares, guildhalls, marketplaces, covered shambles, piazzas, bridges, cottages, malt houses, castles, cemetery tombstones, market houses, universities, shooting ranges, libraries, schools, courthouses, session houses, exchanges, local assembly rooms, playhouses, ballrooms, workhouses, asylums, hospitals, and auditoriums. He preached from many natural formations: rocks, hills, mountainsides, granite boulders, beaches, prehistoric mounds, stone hollows, riverbanks, fields, orchards, meadows, and the shade of convenient trees. This is a not an exhaustive list![4]

In the emerging industrial revolution of the eighteenth century, Wesley was leveraging the power of the third place. He sparked a missional revolution, a renewal movement of the church. Today, a similar movement is coming alive in the fields again.

The phrase "Fresh Expressions" emerged with Anglican Bishop Graham Cray and his team, who produced the *Mission-Shaped Church* (MSC) in 2004. They took the language from the preface to the Declaration of Assent, which states, "The Church of England is part of the One, Holy, Catholic and Apostolic Church, worshipping the one true God, Father, Son and Holy Spirit. It professes the faith uniquely revealed in the Holy Scriptures and set forth in the catholic creeds, *which faith the Church is called upon to proclaim afresh in each generation*" (author emphasis).[5]

The *Mission-Shaped Church* report spread internationally and is credited with transforming the ecclesiology of the Church of England. It has catalyzed the development of thousands of fresh expressions and released similar initiatives in Australia, Canada, mainland Europe, South Africa, the United States, and elsewhere.[6]

A fresh expression is a form of church for our changing culture, established primarily for the benefit of those who are not yet part of any church. These are forms of church that are:

- Missional: birthed by the Spirit to reach not-yet-Christians.

- Contextual: seek to serve the context in an appropriate form to the people in it.

- Formational: focused on making disciples.

- Ecclesial: a full expression of the "church," not a stepping-stone to an inherited congregation.

An essential premise of the movement is that church can happen anywhere bodies have gathered to worship Jesus. It returns us to the possibility of a church that can inhabit buildings but is not dependent on them. It reimagines a parish as a whole place, where church can spring up from every nook and cranny. It envisions the community as an ecosystem, within which there are many habitats where people can gather to grow in love with God and neighbor. A blended ecology that doesn't diminish the importance of a well-designed church building, but equally sees the importance of worshipping God outside of them.

It's a movement of barns and bodies, of guiding and gathering.

Field Exercise

Prayer Caravan

It's time for a field trip! We invite your team to go on a prayer caravan and prepare a field report based on what you discover. This process can be done in a multitude of ways, but the goal is to have a collective insight into where you are and to see the land, the people, the events, and the processes of your area as holy ground to realize the kingdom of God. Imagining possibilities requires that your church is looking and seeing.

- Access a map of your larger community.

- Go over the map and determine an area you would like to cover.

- Invite your team to gather a predetermined location and time.

- Determine who among the group will drive; carpool as much as possible.

- Invite the team to do three things: pray, observe, and encounter.

- As you drive, pray together over your parish.

- Make observations about what you see. Perhaps have someone in each group take notes.

- Leave space for encounter. Do you notice a group of people, a place, a natural phenomenon? Stop and be present for a while.

- Regather and let each team share insights from their time.

- Have someone record the observations and set a date to meet again.

Field Story

Larry Frank, Elder, Tremont UMC in Tremont, Illinois: population 2,500

Located fourteen miles southeast of Peoria, Illinois, Tremont is a small village with a long and proud history. Prior to Abe Lincoln's election to higher office, Tremont played frequent host to Lincoln, the lawyer. He was even famously challenged to a duel in Tremont. Today, the village is largely supported by agriculture and its award-winning school system, and it serves as a bedroom community for commuters who work in Peoria.

A Methodist society and Sunday school was planted in Tremont circa 1890. In 1904, the first sanctuary was built and stood until 2019. The church hit a high point in worship attendance in 2005 after their new sanctuary building was completed. However, worship attendance would decline by over 40 percent from 2006 to 2013.

I was appointed as lead pastor in 2018. During that time and prior to the COVID-19 pandemic, worship attendance grew by over 34 percent, and forty-eight new members joined the church, of which thirty-four were by profession of faith! This early growth was largely through attractional ministry in Sunday morning worship. Before the pandemic, we were in the early stages of moving into the blended ecology of church. The pandemic accelerated the need for this new ecology.

Though we have largely returned to in-person worship, our missional and emerging ministries have been the growth engine of the church. Life Groups, designed for discipleship and accountability and patterned after the Wesleyan class and band meetings, began just prior to our move to online worship. The Life Groups instantly became micro-churches in their own right as participants found creative ways to continue meeting: through Zoom, on back patios, and in the church parking lot as a line of cars backed into a large circle. These micro-churches continue to gather weekly inside and outside the church building, and more are forming regularly!

Another life-giving example comes from an innovative merger. Before the lockdowns, we had two separate ministries that both met on Wednesday nights. Feed the Need was a weekly come-and-go fellowship meal. The Well was an alternative worshipping community that met after the meal in the sanctuary for worship, a short message, and communion. When we returned to the building, we merged the two together into The Table, a dinner church. About fifty people gather weekly for a meal, trusting that Christ will meet us at the table in conversation, music, a short message, and Holy Communion. My favorite part of The Table is watching Communion shared around each table: wives to their husbands, children to their mothers, strangers to new friends. The Table is a beautiful gathering that is multigenerational and a good mix of folk from the inherited church and a growing number of people previously unseen on Sunday mornings.

As we continue to move forward, we trust God for that growth in Tremont through our Sunday morning services as well as these emerging communities. We are currently exploring "messy church" (https://messy-churchusa.org) and a monthly incarnational gathering aimed specifically at reaching men.

CHAPTER 3

Learning to Die Somewhere

The Necessity of Belonging in Rural Churches

I assure you that unless a grain of wheat falls
into the earth and dies, it can only be a single seed.
But if it dies, it bears much fruit. (John 12:24)

A rural church has a particular relationship to a rooted place. Though occasionally forgotten, in most rural communities, this is not a new idea, but the need for rootedness is in stark contrast to the urban transience that plagues rural communities as the next generation moves away. The need for belonging is suppressed, as it is in our culture as a whole.

What happens to people when we are disconnected from our geographical place? What is the effect on churches experiencing dislocation?

As in a marriage, there is a rooted foundation that supports the existence of the body of the church. As thornbushes, to hedge the health of our place, we must relearn how to embody incarnational belonging. Ironically, we must learn how to die in the place we inhabit.[1]

39

Marriage: A Microcosm of Community

Marriage itself is one of the most difficult experiences of human life. The couple is choosing to occupy a common space with a common lifestyle in which every moment involves another person. The spouses see each other's flaws, failures, baggage, and strange behaviors. Marriage is the decision of two people to know each other entirely, every day, for the rest of their complicated existence.

One's relationships with their parents or children, as well as nearly all relationships through the span of one's life, have an optional transience to them. Even though divorce rates are elevated, marriage is one of the only relationships in which full belonging is promised, including with a legal contract.

There is also no other relationship that offers the potential bond of this infinite mingling of two identities. Such a commitment makes possible the sharing of gifts, the combination of skills and personalities that can be mutually beneficial, and the fondness of traversing life and the world with a permanent comrade. If there are four necessary ingredients to community—shared history, shared imagination, proximity, and permanence—marriage offers them all.

Marriage also reveals the struggle in attaining the immense possibility. The daily process of embodying and maintaining those ingredients while persisting through the messiness that emerges anytime you try to exist along another complicated, beautiful, and ambivalent human being is both beautiful and daunting.

The relationship between a congregation and a clergyperson is by analogy an "arranged marriage." Arranged marriages are a type of marital union in which the bride and groom are chosen by persons other than the couple themselves, in many cases by family members or sometimes a professional matchmaker. Arranged marriages have been the dominant route to marriage across history, and arrangements remain common in many regions, notably South Asia and the Middle East.

In some cases, the husband and wife are total strangers. This seems awkward for those of us in the West who talk about "soul mates" and "love at first sight" and who often go through an extensive dating process. Over half of the marriages in the world today are arranged marriages, with a staggeringly low global divorce rate of 6.3 percent.[2] Obviously some forms of arranged marriages are exploitative of women. Forced marriages, particularly those involving children, have been rightfully condemned by the United Nations. For example, in some cultures, death by stoning is still the penalty for adultery or divorce. These patriarchal and oppressive arrangements should be challenged and eliminated.

And yet millions of couples across world history have learned to appreciate and even thrive in arranged marriage unions. Over time, people can learn to love each other, whether they were total strangers or high-school sweethearts. In every marriage, arranged or otherwise, the real marriage begins when the honeymoon is over, and much of marriage work involves learning to give and receive love in healthy ways. It is the infinite mingling of souls that is less about soul mates and more about becoming a kind of household economy, full of interdependent, mutual, self-giving love.

The arranged relationship between a pastor or pastoral team and a congregation has similar interdependence and symbiosis. Whether the clergy were evaluated and interviewed in a call system, grew up through the ranks of the congregation, or were sent to serve the congregation by an episcopacy, this union has been arranged. Somehow, by the grace of God, the pastor(s) and congregation have been brought together in a divine union.

The church is a place of thick relationship and eternal fellowship. The Greek word χοινωνία (*koinonia*) is used to describe the kind of relationship in the church. Fellowship, χοινωνία, can mean partnership or social intercourse or financial benefaction and communion. The word denotes the deepest form of intimacy. The fellowship shared between spouses is similar to the kind of relationships we are expected to share in the church.

Marriage is a microcosm for how community ought to work. However, even as divorce becomes a prevailing option to separate the messiness of human beings, our culture lauds transience as the escape from community.

A Journey Toward Belonging

At one time in my life, I (Tyler) heeded the siren call of transience. I grew up in a small town, and my experience was one of presence becoming absence. Whether through death, divorce, or abandonment, everyone I had known had gone away. I longed for connection, but belonging felt like a fairytale. I got married, moved to the other side of the country, and vowed to never come back. All the places, people, and history were to be archived as a memory in the pursuit of existential ambition.

Then we realized the terror of being completely and utterly alone. Pasadena, California, was our destination, and beyond all of the cultural amenities and geological features, it bolstered the familiar air of absence. Southern California felt like the place to move to so as to run away from broken belonging.

On the warm winter morning of December 12, 2012, my spouse and I hitched a ride to the hospital, since our only mode of transportation—bicycles—was not fit for my spouse's excruciating back pain.

Upon arriving at the hospital, we discovered that the cause of my spouse's three-day debilitation was that she was pregnant; she was nine months pregnant. Yes, we know how children are made. Yes, we know the physiological and biological processes of pregnancy (my spouse's education was in anatomical science). But because of a slew of unprecedented circumstances, we had no idea we were pregnant. We ended that day with our first child.

There are moments when belonging becomes the only thing that matters. The very belonging we shunned and the very connections we ran away from were now the only thing we desired. With no money, no family, and no light at the end of the tunnel, I heard words from my spouse that I desperately imagined were from a nightmare: "We need to move back to Ohio." I always envisioned a life of urban joy. Busy streets, conglomerated access to the best of societal progress, and places with omnipresent opportunity. I considered my future to be akin to a vagabond; I would travel, explore, and never endure the bane of other people. I desired such freedom.

As I considered my future colliding with my shattered past, I had not envisioned ending up in a declining rural community where everyone seems to be a distant cousin of everyone else. Yet I found myself in a place inhabiting the very thing I spent most of my life running from.

Regularly, whether from people who knew me before my rural move or from people meeting me for the first time, I am asked, "Why do you live *out there*?" The connotation is typically elongated with an insinuating emphasis on the second half of the question. The answer is complicated. On the surface, I didn't necessarily choose this location. There was a job opportunity, we were broke, and my decision-making power had been quite diminished after the string of events that brought me to this place. The question is fair, however. Quite literally, some people can't imagine how one can go from Southern California to the remote wilderness of rural northwest Ohio.

My marriage had something to do with it. For a time, we were the only source of connection we had. We experienced what it meant to belong and what it meant to subsume responsibility to another even with the flaws, failures, and messiness. The potential for community—of committing to another, of having a connection mature over time, and of experiencing how loyalty and affection could produce more than the transience of individuality—was found in each other. We were known. We had more in each other than we had alone.

Unfortunately, it is now countercultural to prioritize what is offered collaboratively over what there is to be used and gained from another person. We often live on a quest for individual freedom at the bidding of a life in which we are never home, in which, no matter one's location, we never have a place. As I moved to the countryside, I witnessed the immense history and knowledge that the people carried through one another. While this awareness also fosters small-town gossip, I began to lament how I had no one in my life who knew me my entire life. I had no shared history outside of myself. As I haphazardly found residence in this desolate landscape full of strange people and complicated narratives, I sensed these people had something that my pursuit of progress, liberation, and culture could never offer: belonging.

Rural areas are often defined by their cultural deficit. However, this may reveal more about our culture's blindness than about rural misfortune. These people sure seemed a mess. There also weren't, and still aren't, many amenities in rural areas. Stereotypically, there is nothing to do out here. But there is a lot to be done. I saw, for the first time, people who knew where they were and who they were, together. They carry the generalization of being backward or provincial, but it may simply be because they give credence to what our culture has long forgotten—one another.

When I answer a demeaning question about my current residence, I begin by keeping my children in mind. I hope to provide my children with knowledge, wisdom, and peace. I also hope to provide them with a place. I hope that in their old age they can look upon someone who has seen them and truly known them since their first days. In the end, many of us will die with great stories of adventure and trite memories of the mighty deeds and acquisitions our culture prioritizes. We want to see the world, experience its pleasures, and arrive at a status only possible by traversing the human journey with a sort of homelessness. When my end inevitably comes, I hope that the most important thing I've acquired is the relationships that I held and that held me through a seemingly mediocre life. Shared history. Shared imagination. Proximity. Permanence. These have become my standards. If my life is to find the profound belonging only possible in this limited landscape, then it will require that my flesh one day rot into its ground.

Costly Community

The standards of community are costly. They require one's feet to be firmly rooted, to care about a place with such tenacity that you see to its future by being connected with its past. We often live as if we are the first and last who will be in the places we are. Yet, I have realized that who I am has been in large part determined by those who have come before me and how they chose to live here.

If we are going to pursue this connection and belonging, and if we presume to offer this sacred way of being to the world, we must learn what it means to die in the places we are. I want to die with the satisfaction that I was known and that my contribution to a small place will transcend my own meager existence. I want to enact my life in this small space called nowhere, full of strange people, infinite corn, and chaos. I want to die in a world I was glad to live in, which can only manifest in these few square miles inherited by my consciousness and intimacy.

Our culture often feeds the assumption that the quality of life is determined by luxury, convenience, and access to unhindered individual freedom. Of course, this assumption is best found in the conglomerated metros. To arrive is to have the cool, special, important things only available to those smart enough to detach themselves from messy people and small places where everyone can be known. Shared life is only useful to the extent that it can be escaped.

The alternative disposition of belonging to a place is an important component of the human journey. If the church is meant to bring hope to the world by offering the potential of community, then this rootedness might also be a key ingredient to our work in the world.

As churches, everything we do will be exponentially optimized and meaningfully satisfying if we begin with the standard of belonging.

What does it mean to gather as a church among people who belong together? People are not numbers to signify quantifiable metrics or consumers of content who help pay the bills. When we engage in ministries, we aren't creating a product to help the church grow, but we are offering sustenance for neighbors who depend on one another.

From the belonging perspective, church shopping is inconceivable. Belonging to a place means living within a place with commitment; and commitment persists regardless of what it offers you. Do we consider our relationship to the church in the same way we consider our relationship to a spouse? People leave churches because they don't like the preaching style or the music. At best, they leave because certain ministries are not offered. Church shopping presumes that a deal or an exchange is on the table—two parties trying to exchange value. As soon as the deal does not meet expectation, the relationship is gone. If we spoke of marriage in such a way, a fair bit of skepticism or concern would be warranted. So we must decide what kind of relationship the church is promoting.

Further, church leaders must consider why they do the things they do and how it ought to affect their process. Are our events and philanthropic work meant to check off report boxes? Are we trying to create products for entertaining consumption in order to complete the sale with potential clients? Are we offering the types of content and activities that will make people stick around and, in turn, keep the budget running and statistics favorable?

If so, perceived belonging will only last as long as the circumstances remain. The relational deal will only continue as long as the offer meets expectations. A better alternative is to be so invested in the places we are and the people who inhabit them that everything we do is a genuine response to a place's needs and gifts. It prioritizes meaning and connection, willingly foregoing performative fluff for the sake of the relationship—none of which pays the bills very well.

Pastorally, there is an inclination to sell the church in a pristine, romanticized way. It is tempting to meet a potential participant and present an idealized view of our church. We have hospitality teams and visitor processes to help people think that we have something to offer, that their desires will be thoroughly serviced, and that our church is a great place to be. Then, when ideals are unrealized, those people may have no further reason to stay, unless the reason they are part of the community is based on the rootedness of belonging.

Choosing to Die

Belonging is the first standard that rural churches should consider, if for no other reason than it is more capable of upholding a vision of the universal church than transience can ever touch.

Which brings me to the real answer I give for why I live out here. Because I choose to. I'd rather live in Metamora, Ohio, than Pasadena, California, because I choose to make it home, where roots can grow.

I often meet recent graduates who express their desire to leave rural areas for greener pastures. I try to express how similar that is to uprooting a plant. Often, they don't hear it, just as I didn't hear it when I was their age. They, too, must see for themselves that the grass is the same in those other places. At some point, a person must decide either to keep traveling or to choose to belong to the messiness of where they are.

Once we claim a place as our own, we are choosing to take a certain responsibility for it.[3] Our commitment determines longevity and dedication beyond the circumstances we experience, because those circumstances are our responsibility. We must do something about them, when this commitment extends to the vision of God's kingdom in our communities.

Our belonging within a geographical proximity means we are involved in its development. We don't ask what we can get from the place but what it requires of us. Marriage works when one chooses it. So does belonging. There is no perfect partner, and there is no perfect place. There are only people who choose to belong and choose to build what is in their reach over time.

Belonging requires a sense of permanence, and permanence leads to responsibility. Choosing a place, and choosing to be the presence of Christ in a place, is the equivalent of choosing to die in that place with the same eternal tenacity of a marriage and the same call of discipleship that Jesus commands us. We must nurture the sense that we care deeply for where we are if our churches are to unleash the propensity of being thornbushes in the wilderness of rural communities.

Yet, once we have made this choice, how do we actually belong in this way?

Unless a Grain of Wheat Falls

Jesus said, "unless a grain of wheat falls into the earth and dies, it can only be a single seed. But if it dies, it bears much fruit" (John 12:24). This agrarian analogy is crucial for rural ministry. We choose to love our zip code so much that we weep over it.

For me (Michael), my appointment to a rural congregation was like an arranged marriage. As an urban person, appointed cross-culturally to a rural place, I was meeting my bride for the first time. The rural way of life was somewhat foreign to me and I had a huge learning curve. I was not born in a rural place and had never called a rural place home. Honestly, a rural congregation was my last choice. In congregations with an epis-copal polity, rural churches are often served by retired clergy in their last appointment or by student pastors in their first appointment. When the young pastors grow enough and prove themselves, they get sent to bigger churches.

In those early years, as I was getting to know a new bride, I came to a place where I needed to make a commitment. Was I going to bail with the first opportunity that came my way, or was I going to commit? I've become convinced over the years that you can't have a good relationship when you have a backup plan. If you are keeping other options open on the backburner, something will boil over.

I was deeply influenced by a mentor and seminary professor who told me over lunch, "Michael, find the smallest church in your denomination and serve it with all you have, then you will be faithful to Jesus." His advice is countercultural. For some colleagues in ministry, it probably feels like swapping out spouses every year or so! Some may be angling for the new and improved, and a little bit younger version.

Jesus is calling us to "fall" like a grain of wheat in the soil where we stand. To die to ourselves and to get buried in our place, so the hope of a fruitful harvest can come when we are planted. Honestly, when I arrived at Wildwood, I didn't imagine I'd still be there ten years later. Not because things are all peaches and cream. In fact, it's been ten years of struggling through this arranged marriage. But I've learned that when the honeymoon is over, the real relationship begins.

When the Honeymoon Is Over

In this chapter we've observed that a fruitful rural ministry includes a shared history, shared imagination, proximity, and a commitment to permanence. A commitment to permanence is a commitment to love a people and a place unconditionally.

American agricultural scientist, author, and inventor George Washington Carver famously said, "Anything will give up its secrets if you love it enough."[4] When we love a person or a community for the long haul, secrets will come out, and they won't always be positive. In the recovery community we say, "we are only as sick as our secrets." We must confess them, bring them to light, and make amends for harm we may have caused, to find true healing.

Can we sustain a relationship even when we discover disturbing secrets about the ones we love?

What do you do in an arranged marriage when the other party wants a divorce? What do you do when the honeymoon is over?

I remember that moment clearly. Some of our core leadership had called for a meeting after worship on Sunday. These were people whom I visited in their homes, and I had baptized their grandbabies and conducted funerals for their loved ones. They had been putting up with my long-winded sermons for almost five years. They had accepted that I was not a sit-in-the-office pastor and that I saw the community as my parish.

But things became strained when we started having church in fields, dog parks, and nature trails with people who didn't go to church. They got more strained when we started spearheading racial reconciliation marches, pulpit swaps with Black preachers, interracial revivals, and a gathering in the Martin Luther King Jr. building. The final straw for some was when a Black Pentecostal church plant needed a place to call home and I suggested that place should be us. Even more disturbing for some was that we had committed not to charge them anything, but to donate the space and electricity, as a way of making reparations for our role in preserving racism and segregation. We didn't want a business contract, rather a covenantal relationship.

"Those Blacks have their church, and we have ours. That's how it's always been, and that's how God wants it," said one longtime member. Another led a mutiny after calling my biracial granddaughter a "half-breed" and said that we should not encourage our daughter to "mix the species," as this was "against God's word."

They gathered in the meeting to share their concerns openly. "Pastor, I remember your first sermon was called 'The Arranged Marriage,' and you told us we would want a divorce one day. That day has come," said one of the elders of the church. For over an hour they fired away with their critiques and complaints. When it was over, those people left, but another group was on standby to surround me in love and prayer.

Ultimately, the mutiny led to half the congregation leaving and putting our church in an unstable place. I wondered if I had truly worn out my welcome and if it might be better to pack up and head down the road. Through a deep period of soul searching and seeking the wisdom of mentors and friends, I ultimately decided that my commitment to this place was worth fighting for. It was even worth dying for. A pastor is sent not simply to a congregation but to a community. A congregation that holds onto anything that obstructs "loving God and neighbor" is not bringing health to a community but infecting it with sickness.

Belonging cannot be for an exclusive few who know the secret code to enter the gated community. We must create communities of belonging in which all people are welcome, regardless of race, age, or orientation. It's not the dirty little secret of rural congregations only; any congregation—made up of people who are "very good" and wounded by sin—can harbor evil and "anti-God" tendencies. When rural congregations become a stronghold of racism, nationalism, or sexism, Jesus is coming back to flip those tables every time.

Rural congregations must discover for themselves that Jeremiah's logic is true, that it is indeed in seeking the well-being of the place where you are, that you will find your own well-being (Jeremiah 29:7). If any group of people in our community is marginalized, suffering, or excluded, the whole health of the community is compromised. If the church is truly a sign, instrument, and foretaste of God's kingdom, then we exist not only for ourselves but for all people. We need to reflect that great heavenly multitude, that no one could count, from every nation, from all tribes and peoples and languages, standing before the throne and before the Lamb (Revelation 7:9). We must keep praying Jesus's prayer—"on earth as it is in heaven"—until it comes to pass.

I learned after the honeymoon that love is a choice we make in a marriage. Even when the other party is unfaithful. When the honeymoon is over, and the proverbial stuff hits the fan, that's when the real adventure of marriage begins. Engaging in healthy conflict, speaking the truth in love, and working through differences are all parts of long-term relationships. Many times, we can come through it stronger on the other side.

When we commit to love each other, even in our unloveliness, that is *koinonia*, that is the church.

Field Exercise

Dream Session

Review the data from a statistical analysis of your community. Now revisit your findings from your prayer caravan to create an integrated field report. Summarize and review the findings together as a team.

1. Did you learn anything new about your community from using a data tool to collect demographics and lifestyles?

2. How did the data about your community agree or disagree with your experience in the prayer caravan?

3. What did these exercises confirm about your understanding of your context?

4. How did these exercises challenge or surprise you about your context?

5. What needs can you identify so far?

6. How might your congregation be able to love and serve people at their point of need?

As you consider the nature of your place, are you willing to take ownership for it? Perhaps you encountered some discouraging patterns; possibly you were surprised by unique arrangements, configurations, data, or historical narratives that nurture a sense of pride. In examining this information, do you see this place as yours?

Serving the people and the place you are begins with loving it, even the parts that may be difficult to love.

Now, invite your team to share imaginations for what could be in your context.

Let these be your framing questions:

What is? The SWOT analysis exercise might be helpful here. Based on all you know about your community, what are some of your Strengths, Weaknesses, Opportunities, and Threats?

What could be? Dreaming big, what visions do you see for you church and community? How could your resources, strengths, and opportunities manifest in new ways?

What will be? What steps could you take next? Who will do it? What will you do next? Who will do what by when?

Field Story

Calla Gilson, Laity, Lead Coordinator for the Discipleship Initiative (among 161 churches) in the Northwestern Ohio Evangelical Lutheran Church in America

We live in a region of the United States that some refer to as "fly over" country, or the place you drive through on your way to somewhere else. Fifth-, sixth-, and seventh-generation rural communities are rooted to caring for the land and the people living in the "in-between." We are a rural region with 77.8 percent of our parishes serving communities of fewer than 50,000.[5] And in each of those communities, farmers and children of farmers have a relationship with this sacred geography that is uniquely rooted to the land.

For us, the work of nurturing new Christian communities in our rural setting is not something trendy, imported, or programmed. It is the people of our places reclaiming what it means to care for our people, just as we care for the land. When we gather with leaders of our parishes, they are proud to share the values of their place as the fertile space from which new Christian communities could grow. We're the great-grandchildren of folk who met in Grange halls to play euchre, whose grandparents donated the farm ground where the church building was constructed, and whose parents taught their kids about care for creation in 4-H clubs that continue to meet in the basements of our country churches. When asked to describe the strengths of life together here, members of our congregations rated our work to address social concerns and interact with the local community as the most vital.[6]

There's a song in the hymnal that we like to sing in rural Northwest Ohio. It begins with giving thanks and praise to God for the blessing of creation and the gift we have been given to care for this land. The praise overflows in diligent work, providing for the community, and partnering with God to ensure that everyone is cared for. And as the good things of this place are shared, the people confess those blessings and return to praise God.

> *Praise and thanksgiving, God, we would offer for all things living, you have made good: harvest of sown fields, fruits of the orchard, hay from the mown fields, blossom, and wood.* (*ELW*, "Praise and Thanksgiving," 689)

It is great joy to gather innovative lay folk and clergy from across the synod to dream about what it looks like to celebrate the gifts and meet the needs of their contexts through uniquely incarnational ministries that look like the love of Jesus we sing about. We are currently walking alongside forty-one people as they host dinner church in local restaurants and barns, gather at wineries for spiritual conversations, grow community gardens with families, and nurture new communities that reflect the seasons of life here in rural Northwest Ohio. In the process, we are reclaiming what it means for us to be from this place and care for this place in ways that renew the community and all of creation.

CHAPTER 4

Circles That Heal

Recovering the Art of Neighborliness

Philip found Nathanael and said to him, "We have found the one Moses wrote about in the Law and the Prophets: Jesus, Joseph's son, from Nazareth."
Nathanael responded, "Can anything from Nazareth be good?"
Philip said, "Come and see." (John 1:45-46)

Our friends in Royal, Florida, who trace their ancestry back to African royalty have taught us a different way to understand life.

Ubuntu: A person is a person through other persons. There is an African anthropological concept that highlights the interdependency of humanity. Historically, Africans are a collectivistic people who emphasize that all individuals are woven together in a single interconnected organism. Life is communal, and our personhood is communally formed. Life is not linear but cyclical, a rhythm of movements. In the circle of life, even a small act of harm or healing affects the entire world. Our humanity is inextricably linked in a bundle of life with all others.

This African notion of self emphasizes personhood as a manifestation of community—a socially constructed self. A person's state of wellness is bound to a web of relationships. Connectedness, belonging, and social acceptance are emphasized rather than individuation. *Ubuntu* highlights community as the goal of life. Wounds are not created in isolation; they are created in community, and they can only truly be healed in community.

The well-being of our neighbor is somehow bound up in our own well-being. If a neighbor is suffering, shunned, injured, or in need, we are too. If a neighbor is thriving, so are we. Perhaps this is what Jesus is modeling for us when he tells us that we will see him in the hungry, thirsty, naked, sick, incarcerated, and the stranger (Matthew 25:31-45). We will find Jesus in the most disadvantaged and vulnerable in our community. Jesus saw himself in them. Perhaps we should too.

In "Manifesto: The Mad Farmer Liberation Front,"[1] Wendell Berry writes, "Be afraid to know your neighbors and to die." Recovering the art of neighborliness is a radical call to know and "love our neighbor," and to seek their well-being. Loving our neighbor well generally involves some self-death. This is true of all our neighbors, not just an exclusive group with whom we are closest. Jesus radically expands the idea of neighbor to include all people, even the ones we might consider unclean, an enemy, or a despised "other" of a different race (Luke 10:25-37).

Edward O. Wilson was an American biologist, naturalist, two-time Pulitzer Prize–winning writer, and is known as the "father of biodiversity." Wilson describes our natural affinity for life as "biophilia," the core essence of our humanity that links us together with all living species.[2] In essence, love of our place and the life within it is a species trait of human beings made in the image of God. Biodiversity refers to the biological variety and variability of life on our planet and helps us understand our delicate relationship with our ecosystems.

Bioregionalism, a term coined by Allen Van Newkirk in 1975, suggests that political, cultural, and economic systems are more sustainable and just if they are organized around naturally defined areas called bioregions. Understanding our context as a bioregion, an ecologically and geographically defined area, can help us approach forming a harmony between human culture and the natural environment. The well-being of a community is also linked to the ecosystem and how we live with the land.

Loving our neighbor includes taking on a posture of placefulness. Jenny Odell—an artist, writer, and professor at Stanford University—describes placefulness as sensitivity and responsibility to the historical (what happened here) and ecological (who and what lives, or lived, here). Odell describes bioregionalism as a model for how we might be able to think about our place again.[3]

Places are not merely physical space holders; they are living, breathing ecosystems. Places have a distinct web of relationships. Places are made of particular flowers, birds, insects, water sources, temperatures, climates, and mammals. When human beings are part of those ecosystems, the ecosystems include webs of customs, languages, cultures, and meaning systems. One way to love our neighbor is to love the place that we share and depend on together for life.

Ubuntu can help us find a framework for neighboring well, but it can also help us recover the true implications of the incarnation of Jesus Christ.

Going Particular to Get Universal

If you want to get to the universal, you have to take the path of the particular. This is what's truly radical but rarely understood about the incarnation. By taking on flesh, Jesus linked himself in a bundle of life with all humanity. He linked himself with a creation that was both very good and wounded. He entered into the interconnected matrix of human relationships. He entered into the joy, the struggle, the pain, and even the sin. He became sin, so that we might be healed (2 Corinthians 5:21). He took a place in the circle of life, and he took our place on the cross.

Jesus entered particularity, to heal universally.

Jesus from Nazareth. He came to a particular time, to a particular family, and to a particular place. That place, Nazareth, was rural. It was a forgotten place. A place you went through accidentally to get where you were going. But Jesus's communal identity was formed in that place.

Jesus was a country boy. He was a rural person who came from a rural place, the little hamlet of Nazareth (probable population: 400). Jesus was known as "Joseph's son from Nazareth," which elicited the following jest from the would-be follower Nathanael, "Can anything from Nazareth be good?" (John 1:46). Most of Jesus's ministry took place in the rural context. And Jesus spoke in a language and in parables contextually appropriate for rural people.

One of Jesus's notable healing miracles took place in Capernaum, which is called a "city" (Luke 4:31) with approximately 1,500 people. As soon as Jesus and his disciples left the synagogue, ministry broke out. They went over to Simon Peter's house, where the incredible power to heal even in-laws was unleashed! Word spread, and suddenly the whole town was on Peter's front porch. They brought to Jesus all who were sick, mad, or addicted, and Jesus healed them one by one (Mark 1:28-34).

Who knew that ministry could take place in ordinary places such as on a front porch? Gathering in the rural places—like a church in the wild. Today we call communities like this "fresh expressions": church for people who don't go to church. This was a fresh expression of healing, outside the centers of religious and imperial power.

Jesus's love took on particularity. Jesus didn't just love people in general; he loved particular persons. Real people with real names. People who were both very good and wounded. Real people who lived in real communities. Communities with real assets and real liabilities.

Jesus started small. He created small circles of people, whom he knew intimately, and they knew him. These circles were little ecosystems of grace where people found healing from their wounds. Many times, the implications of their healing had communal dimensions. As they were healed, they healed others. Entire places seemed to have been left healed in the wake of Jesus's ministry, but usually they started small (Mark 1:28-34).

As pastors, we know that sometimes it's easier to love the idea of people, rather than the people themselves. Particular people are messy. Particular relationships with our neighbors are challenging. But healing cannot simply be an idea. It must become incarnate. We must enter into real relationships with particular people. We must embrace our place in the circle of life.

This particularity is what collectivistic cultures get that we rugged individualists largely fail to understand. This is why most places have largely failed at the art of neighborliness. It requires us to cultivate circles that heal. Rural communities are particularly wired for these kinds of circles because we can in some sense know all our neighbors. We can enter into smallness and particularity that is more challenging in urban settings with anonymous larger populations. But it's precisely in going particular that there are universal implications.

Importance for Rural Churches

Rural churches have the unfortunate blessing of being a small sample size. We can know everyone with an intimacy and proximity that is impossible in dense, urban, or suburban areas. Within the several square miles of a community's vicinity, it is literally possible to know everyone. The downside is that we also get to know everyone with intimacy and proximity. The sentiment of suburban isolation or being lost in the urban crowd can sound appealing after you have seen the tenacity with which rural communities can implode with gossip. We ought not to see this intimacy as inherently good or bad. What we should see is that the small demographic of rural communities offers two unique outcomes in our pursuit of belonging.

In ages past, this was always seen as a benefit. Neighbors were necessary to survival, and not just economically. Sure, there are the tropes of sharing a cup of sugar, but the interdependence necessary to be able to eat, survive, endure harsh winters, and deal with the traumas and tragedies that ripple through small communities with incessant velocity was what kept the small tribes of rural areas alive. Being able to know one another meant being able to endure the best and worst of life with one another.

The human person has a capacity when maintaining interpersonal relationships. Accounts vary. Some say 150 relationships, but the common claim is 200 relationships. In this respect, the small demographic is an advantage for being the church; we can literally serve and see to the shalom of each member of our place.

Yet, the small cohort is also a disadvantage. If you can have a community of 200 people, but you have one million to choose from, you greatly increase the odds that you are going to like all the people involved. In urban settings, the search for community becomes a bit like dating. You search around, court potential connections, and then maintain relationships with the people who are most like you. Not only are you able to escape or isolate from people you don't want to know, but also you have many more options.

This brings us to the second factor of belonging in rural communities with small demographics: you can't choose your neighbors.

A rural church, therefore, is less likely to have a community of people who all think the same. The neighbors with a dozen broken cars in their front lawn and the wealthy farmer with a pristine lawn and gated driveway both must be neighbors. And in rural communities, they are both just as essential to the health of the place. In a rural community, we need each and every one of them.

John Wesley understood this dynamic in the church. In observing the "catholic spirit" of the church, he stated, "Though we do not think alike, can we not love alike?"[4] While most rural churches are not known for being racially diverse, they cannot avoid mental, emotional, existential, economic, generational, and ideological diversity. On a given Sunday, there may be hillbillies and hippies; collared conservatives and high-brow liberals; industrial farmers and old-school homesteaders; and most people are a bit of all of them at the same time.

Rural churches cannot afford to ask, "What is your political perspective?" as some sort of metal detector for letting people in or turning them away. We don't get to choose who belongs to our communities.

The question rural churches must ask is, "What do we need to do so that we can all sit in the room together?" Because we can love alike even if we don't all think alike. There needs to be a common bond, a common vision, and a shared imagination that holds us together despite the tenuous diversity that could tear us apart. Larger places might able to create unity without diversity. Our small demographics force us to do the hard, yet beautiful work of creating unity within diversity. We are just a bunch of humans learning to belong to our place together. When we start there, we can all sit at the table and continue to walk together, learn together, and grow as a result of our unique experiences together.

There are circles that heal in the rural church, we know, because we found them for ourselves.

Take Off Your Shoes . . . Holy Ground

I (Michael) can remember when we drove off a main highway down a winding dirt road. We were in the middle of nowhere. No post office. No stop lights. No gas station. And most certainly, no strip malls! At the fork in the dirt road, we saw the familiar site of a cross on a white, wood-sided church.

The building was constructed in the one-room church design that was typical in the 1880s. The sanctuary functioned as worship space, a Sunday school classroom, and the pastor's office. Then, of course, we noticed the spot where the outhouse once stood. Later the congregation added a small kitchen, a few Sunday school classrooms, and a bathroom with indoor plumbing. Then came the fellowship hall addition, a single room, lined with long tables for the potluck.

We entered the sanctuary for the first time late on a Sunday afternoon, at the invitation of the congregation. The special guest that day was a local musical group called the Over-all Gang, and they played a vast array of instruments, many of which would be unfamiliar to the urban eye and ear. Then I noticed. They were barefoot! Not just the musicians, but the dozen or so members of the congregation. Most of them had taken off their shoes and slid them under the pews.

This was worlds away from my impoverished neighborhood in Ocala, Florida, known to the locals as the "white ghetto." I grew up with a corner store, baseball field, recreation center, restaurants, and of course several churches, all within walking distance, and none of them used zithers in their worship. In some ways, I felt like I had crossed into a different reality. My wife, Jill, and our blended family of eight children felt like all eyes were on us. Not only because we arrived late (we got lost on the rough back roads with no street signs and no GPS) but also because we were the new pastoral family with this congregation.

The Holy Spirit nudged us, so we took off our shoes and joined the community. We started to feel the music, to sway a little bit, and then even to clap and raise our hands—like halfway, you know, the conservative Methodist thing to do!

In between songs, someone from the Over-all Gang would go to "testifying." These short narratives in between songs had a similar structure: I've been through a struggle, it was hard, but God is faithful! Then there were shouts, amens, and more music. The musical celebration, which they referred to as a "sing," continued for a couple hours. These rituals had a long history, reaching back to the soil layer of insurgent forms of Christianity we referenced earlier. They enacted dissent and meaning and subversively carried forward defining stories down through generations.

Then we crossed over into the one-room fellowship hall, a much newer shed-like building, where covered dishes were sitting on long tables. We sat with these people who seemed strange to us, and we ate together, and then something sacred began to happen. People came to introduce themselves, telling us the different dishes they brought and what we needed to make sure and try. The spread was impressive, just about every kind of meat you can imagine, all fried, then a mix of collard greens and other vegetables, each mixed with bacon or pork of some kind. But the dessert table literally "took the cake" as even more fantastic.

We listened to people's stories and learned their names. It was particularly challenging to follow the genetic threads in the conversation because every person there was somehow related. Each one descended from the great matriarch, who sat smiling gently at the head of the table. When the time was right, I made my way to sit beside her and ask her name. I felt like I was somehow bowing my knee to the bishop of this strange land. Her words were graceful, joyful, and full of southern charm. By "kissing her ring," we were somehow being brought into the family.

Slowly, they began to bring me—a city slicker who didn't know to take my shoes off and had never seen nor heard of a zither or an autoharp—into the sacred fold. In just a couple weeks, we would return not as guests but as the appointed clergy. Thus began a journey of incarnation into the rural world. Thus, we began a journey of earning the title pastor. We were entering into the particularity of a real place, with real people, with real names, real stories, and real wounds.

There, I was enfolded in a circle of healing. A circle that shattered my stereotypes, deflated my ego, and put me back together as a more whole person.

The Circle of Life

I (Michael) am a 1980s baby. I think every generation since the 1940s has their formative Disney film, and ours was *The Lion King*. The now classic film opens with a song called "Circle of Life":

> But all are agreed as they join the stampede.
> You should never take more than you give. . . .

Indeed, we live in the circle of life. I never understood the meaning of these words until I learned to live incarnationally with rural people. They taught me that what I once considered to be weird and outdated ways and rituals, are faithful acts of Christian subversion. They sing, testify, and dance their faith. This sustains their hope, as the stampede of extraction, commoditization, and violence tramples the land. They hold onto the decency to never take more than they give. In their community, meeting relational felt needs is part of the art of neighborliness. They live in harmony with the land, and by their labor and sweat, we have food on our tables.

Now, life is not all experienced like a bowl of cherries in the rural land. I was surprised to discover all the same problems exist there as in the city, but sometimes in different forms. Alcoholic fathers still beat their kids, cousins still commit suicide, and people still sell their bodies in exchange for drugs. Much of this trafficking activity takes place in the church parking lot, since it's the only neutral community space for miles around.

But there's also healing here too. We build circles of trust in which conversation and care can take place. This is where Jesus does his best work, just like in Capernaum. In the isolation, community is a form of resistance. In the rural church we create space for connection, and this can take place in informal spaces, not just in the church sanctuary.

Relational Con-Artistry

How do you sell the Eiffel Tower?

In May of 1925, Victor Lustig, the deputy director of the Ministry of Postal Services and Telecommunications in France, sent an urgent message to all scrap metal companies in the area to meet him immediately. Only six showed up. There was an elaborate meal full of wine as Lustig explained that the government needed to knock down the Eiffel Tower and scrap it. However, it was a huge secret, and a deal needed to be made that evening.

Lustig then began the bidding process for this valuable government contract. Within the group was the owner of a newer company, and this was an opportunity to put his business on the map. He won the bid for the equivalent of one million dollars.

There were a few problems. Lustig didn't work for the government, there was no such thing as the deputy director of the Ministry of Postal Services and Telecommunications, and none of this scheme was actually real.

Victor Lustig was a con artist, and this was one of the largest scams ever to happen in history. Lustig actually sold the Eiffel Tower twice. As soon as he got the money, he left for the United States.

What makes this possible? How is someone capable of selling the Eiffel Tower, not logistically, but in willingness to subvert relationships with other human beings?

The people involved in Lustig's selling of the Eiffel Tower were simply objects from which to get something. If there was any interest in these gullible contractors as human beings, it had to be pushed to the side. They had to become two-dimensional objects to be used for personal gain. It's egocentrism at its finest. We all do it. Like the first-person viewpoint of a role-playing video game, we live as if we are surrounded by a bunch of NPCs (non-player characters) who are simply there to catalyze our stories. Self-interests become unrestrained as we exploit and use the world around us for our own needs. There is no dependence or arrangement of loyalty. When it's done, we just get on a boat and sail to the United States, leaving the other characters forever in the past.

The kind of belonging central to community requires the opposite. Community is the invitation to be real; and real is not always glamorous, but it is beautiful.

As churches, if we are going to foster healthy, connected, thriving relational communities, we can choose to be scammers or we can choose to be real. The journey is not for the faint of heart; for this kind of belonging requires vulnerability. However, if we are truly set to enrich and enliven the state of our rural communities, this is an absolute necessity.

Revitalization begins here. No tweak, ministry, or sermon matters without choosing to belong and actually doing it. So, if we are going to embark on this journey, what does this holistic, vulnerable belonging look like?

Rural Church as a Circle of Healing

We've been learning that church community can spring up anywhere under the right conditions. For example, when we went to the next town up the road and asked the servers in the diner what church would look like for them, it turns out that it looked like church happening there in the restaurant where they worked, over tables loaded with barbecue.

In that third place, people who couldn't or didn't want to attend church could have open conversations about the joys and struggles in their life. We centered these conversations around "Jesus stories," simple little retellings about something Jesus said or did, and then we asked people what they thought about it. People who were never quite comfortable getting "preached at" on Sunday mornings found space to ask questions and join a sermonic conversation.

People who weren't comfortable coming into the church sanctuary, but enjoyed a good brisket or sliced pork sandwich, could sip some sweat tea with their friends as they thought about the story. They could wrestle with the implications of the story in their own life if they thought it might be true. It's amazing how people would honestly share about their deepest moments of pain and struggle, just by reflecting on the stories of Jesus. It's also amazing how time and time again, people expressed a deep sense of healing, by simply articulating their grief or doubts in an unfiltered way.

In the span of one year, our little congregation of 12 grew to almost 100. This was miraculous; we had the highest percentage increase in attendance for our denomination in the whole state of Florida! But then again, we did double the congregation on our first Sunday with our family of eight kids. But the people who call rural areas home taught me that "church" needs three critical attributes: church needs to be *accessible, safe,* and *real.*

Let's take a look at these three attributes.

- **Accessible:** These communities form in the normal spaces where people gather and speak plain truth for plain people. The only requirement for membership is a "desire to flee the wrath to come." This church is close, in our neighborhood, and speaks a common language, just as Jesus did when he "made his home among us" (John 1:14).

- **Safe:** These communities meet in small, intimate groups. All people from every walk of life are welcome, and harmful behaviors are not tolerated. It's a place of healing, not harm, an environment of grace, an inclusive space where the "good news" is made available to all (Luke 4:18-19).

- **Real:** People are invited to come to terms with and express their brokenness. We can ask some version of "How goes it with your soul?" People are invited to name their woundedness in a community of reciprocity and mutual support. They process their pain in uncensored language, with prayer that brings real healing (James 5:16).

These small communities are places of embodied hospitality. A community that is accessible, safe, and real can give people space to express their struggles and find healing. They make room for every person to play a part in the circle of life. The rural church sustains us in this way. Indeed, rural churches are critical arteries for the whole body of Christ.

Circles that heal can best occur informally and can happen anywhere: barn parties, farmers markets, fishing holes, hunting expeditions, yard sales, harvest fields, bars, barbecue joints, and the list goes on; use your imagination. Sometimes, we need to create those spaces, in the rhythms and spaces where people gather for life.

Sometimes, we need to intentionally construct these circles within our pre-existing spaces. Circles that heal can happen in church buildings; people have been experiencing healing in inherited congregations for many centuries. In fact, in the rural congregation, the building can be our greatest asset. It may be the only communal space for many miles. Rural congregations are one of the few permanent stakeholders in the community. In whatever ways the world has changed around us, our church building still stands, as a testament to something solid, ancient, and resilient. Enshrined in that space is the collective story of a people and a place. Sometimes it's even in the stained glass or the architecture. The rural congregation's building is subversive, a guardian of the Tel.

But we do need to rethink those spaces. In worship, we have to be careful of secret gate codes and insider-only rituals. Nothing kills intended hospitality faster than constantly telling outsiders that they are outsiders until they look like us. We want to create a welcoming environment where strangers can become friends, and that may require us not to be so beholden to our preferences and familiarities. The common disposition is that "outsiders" come to our churches like guests in our home. They must abide by our expectations before being accepted. Yet, the most hospitable approach might just be to view our spaces as their spaces. From our architecture, decoration, communication, setup, dialogue, and actions we are telling them where they stand and who is in control. We might as well tell everyone who enters that we all, together, stand on holy ground and that one of the primary characteristics of holy ground is that no one owns it. Whether one is a guest or a matriarch, this is everyone's space, together. If you entered your church building or came to a service as a stranger, would you feel like you already belonged, or would you feel a bit weirded out, possibly even unwelcomed?

Beyond the common use of church spaces, however, we can also use spaces in the church facility for smaller intimate gatherings that are more conversational. Forums of grace where people can speak and be heard. Where people feel safe enough to take the bandages off their wounds.

Finally, sometimes a circle that heals is just a posture we carry with us. We are "little Christs," temples of the Holy Spirit, and microcosms of the new creation. The more we faithfully seek to embody loving God and loving neighbor, the more we can leave a trail of healing in our wake. The small acts of kindness and love have cosmic consequences in the circle of life. *Ubuntu*: We are persons through other persons, and through authentic relationships we can spread goodness through the whole bundle of life. Our little mustard seed acts of faith can grow into a kingdom tree, where all the birds can find rest (Matthew 13:31-32).

All situations and moments are an opportunity to create circles of deep, rooted trust and belonging where we aren't afraid to know our neighbors and to die. This is the key to the art of neighborliness.

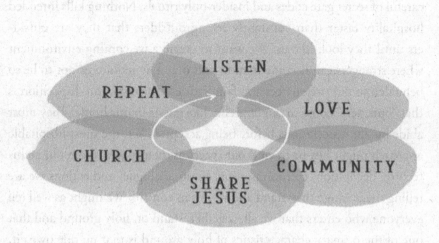

Field Exercise

Exploring the "Listening First Journey"

The "listening first journey"[5] we follow in the Fresh Expressions movement is a way to cultivate new Christian communities. It also helps us avoid attempts to "franchise" successful ideas and strategies that may not be contextually appropriate for your congregation. It is a way of cultivating new forms of church that are: accessible, safe, and real. Read through the journey with your team and answer the questions for each step.

Listen

We begin with a double act of listening. This involves hearing what God is speaking through Christian tradition and in the context. We can spend time together in prayer, studying Scripture, sharing about what we hear God saying, and developing that in conversation with the wider tradition of the church. We will prayerfully inhabit the spaces where God calls us to join what the Spirit leads. We must actually be present with the people, in their places, joining in their common practices.

Listening involves learning the local language, customs, assumptions, hopes, and dreams. It is our spade, in the contextual work of excavating our Tel. It requires seeking to understand a community's customs, rituals, and values. How do they make a living? How do they communicate? By what means? What do they watch? What do they listen to? What is their pain? Where are the life-affirming tendencies? What is wounded and in need of healing? What is good news to them? How do these cultural factors intersect with the gospel of Jesus Christ?

Love

Love flows organically from a sincere desire to be present and listen to people. Loving is not about doing something for or to a group of people who need what we have. It is a mutual exchange of blessing. There is no hidden agenda. Love is the end. Love is the goal. Love is the way. Sometimes fresh expressions will form from our loving of others; sometimes they will not. Love is not a means to an end. Love is focused on the messy activity of building relationships. In this relational connectivity we can cultivate circles that heal.

Our call to "heal" the community must be built on the foundation of meaningful relationships. We are on holy ground, welcomed in, doing life with them, and shalom is bursting forth. From those relationships, we can release a flood of healing that affects the land, the economy, and the wider circle of life.

How can we grow in loving and serving our community? Where are the sore spots that need healing?

Community

As we listen and love, relationships start to grow. A *koinonia* community (described in chapter 3) begins to form. *Koinonia* refers to communion, interpenetration, fellowship, and sharing in a gift jointly contributed (Philippians 2:1).

Community cannot be downloaded or franchised. The franchised church is like an assembly line, in which professional clergy oversee an organization that provides religious goods and services. We mean community in the sense of *Ubuntu*, a profound sense of connectedness, in which the life-giving community experiences the healing of our isolation.

Where are we experiencing deeper levels of community with those outside the church?

Share Jesus

Our community development work is rooted in following and trusting in Jesus's faithfulness, which motivates our vocation to share his love in the world. We can say with E. Stanley Jones, "I am convinced that the only kind of a world worth having is a world patterned after the mind and spirit of Jesus."[6] Our work in practicing life in God's kingdom involves evangelism. In Luke 10:1-9, "proclaiming the kingdom" accompanies healing, eating, and abiding together. In the evangelical church's gospel, some reduce the idea of evangelism to saving souls for heaven when we die, but this is not what we mean by sharing Jesus here. Every dimension of cultivating (and transforming) a place economy is evangelism.

We come to faith, grow in our faith, and share our faith in one continuous rhythm. When we share faith through authentic relationships, the community grows in depth and strength. When Jesus is the central relationship in a community, it can sustain all kinds of challenges, even at the gates of hell. As we move beyond whatever work, passion, hobby, practice, or social interest forming the particular community (fresh expression), the activities shared together are anchored in Christ.

How are we sharing Jesus in word and in relationship?

Church

As we go about this work of cultivating God's kingdom, we organically find contextual churches springing up from the native soils. Church happens not only when we are "gathered" in one particular locale, but also when we are "scattered" across the community. We see this rhythm of a church gathered and scattered, collected and distributed, Jerusalem and Antioch, deep roots and wild branches (Acts 11, 15; Romans 11:16-24). We think of each of the spaces where community can form as habitats in a larger parish ecosystem.

The historic marks of the church—one, holy, catholic, and apostolic—in the Nicene Creed serve as a guide. There is a oneness to a church, unified by the common center, which is Jesus himself. There is a holiness to a church where people are authentically sharing their struggles and leaning into the power of God for transformation. There is a catholicity to a church connected across space and time, and staying in conversation with the wider church tradition. There is a mission to this church, sent like the early apostles and circuit riders across the rural landscape, engaging people in the place where they spend most of their time.

How can we see church starting to form with people currently outside our church?

Repeat

Multiplication is inherent to cultivating disciples in this way. We are cultivating little Christian communities, like barns across rolling fields of grain. As people come to faith, they are empowered by the Spirit to share Jesus in a way that's unique to them and their work, hobbies, practices, and relational networks.

How are we thinking about multiplication?

Field Story

Allen Stanton, Executive Director of the Turner Center for Rural Vitality at University of Tennessee Southern

A few years ago, I moved to Pulaski, Tennessee, in order to become the director of the Turner Center for Rural Vitality. At the time, the Turner Center was part of Martin Methodist College, a small, rural, denominational school. The then-president of our institution gave me a fairly broad mandate: we want to work with rural churches to help rural communities.

In July of 2021, Martin Methodist College—and with it, the Turner Center—was acquired by the University of Tennessee, becoming the newest, smallest campus in the university system. With the transition, I also became the Chief of Mission Integration and Outreach, overseeing the whole of the university's community and economic development work. Our work now encompasses a broad variety of rural development initiatives, several of which work with faith communities.

The Turner Center is a particularly attractive place from which to work, for a couple reasons. First, the school itself is rural, primarily serving first-generation, rural students. When I talk about the importance of cultivating thriving rural communities, I'm echoing a larger culture on our campus. Second, because we're located in a rural community, we have a better understanding of the opportunities and challenges facing rural places, and we understand the potential for rural congregations to offer meaningful leadership.

In many rural communities, congregations are some of the few permanent anchor institutions. Metropolitan areas tend to have a plethora of hospitals, philanthropies, non-profits, corporate headquarters, and universities, which can collaborate to do innovate work. Many rural places lack these pivotal institutions.

Rural communities do have an abundance of rural congregations. Rural congregations tend to have a larger cross-section of the community; they are trusted institutions, and the members are typically dedicated to the institution. They also know the strengths of rural places—and there are many strengths in rural communities—in a way that lets them offer a profound witness to what God's kingdom is doing.

The day-to-day life of a center at a public institution is focused on economic development. I've found that rural churches are an essential partner in that work. We train congregations to expand access to health care, leveraging the strong social ties in their church. They provide access to broadband to students who might not otherwise have it. Churches that have participated in our cohorts—small churches of around thirty people—have surrounded a family and lifted them out of homelessness. They provide mentorship and workforce development, expanding the imagination of what's possible for students.

Community development is profound work that transforms communities, leveraging the existing assets through low-cost, high-impact practices. As a pastor, I also know that this is evangelism. This is helping communities recognize and participate in the social and economic structures of God's kingdom.

CHAPTER 5

Preaching Non-Downloadable Content

Jesus told the crowds all these things in parables;
without a parable he told them nothing. (Matthew 13:34 NRSV)

So far, these ideas about belonging and community development may sound ideal, but what do we actually do? Transparency about rural decline is necessary, and the state of rural churches demands our attention and candor. We also must take seriously the intrinsic capability of rural places and their churches. While hope and imagination can invigorate passion, understanding the identity, essence, and purpose of rural churches leaves many gaps to be filled.

What does a body of thornbushes do? How do we incarnate this metaphor? And, as is a particular curiosity among churches seeking revitalization, what happens to our content—our services of Word and Table, our events, and the programs or affinity groups found in rural churches?

A different approach is necessary.

Rethinking "Church Growth"

Preach the good news and administer the sacraments. Depending on denominational identity, this is the core description of ordained pastoral leadership.

During the final quarter of the twentieth century, the churches that thrived would be the churches that were the most attractive. Churches became known for having the best content—namely, worship, sermons, study groups, and programs for all ages.

Churches, depending on social location (usually suburban) and long-tenured charismatic leadership, that could offer this content excellently would grow to become large. As churches grew larger, they could tap the wealth of donors to build bigger buildings with larger seating. Large churches developed wondrous children ministries and hospitality that could compete with the best of the service industry. Walking across a large parking lot into a towering building, shaking dozens of hands, grabbing a decadent coffee or lemonade, and taking a wide cushion seat in a dimly lit auditorium was as attractive experience on any given Sunday.

Not many churches could follow suit (for many reasons, including location, economic class, aging adults, and culture wars). Criticism was inevitable. This emphasis on attraction sometimes drifted into entertainment rather than discipleship. Church families in some places traded intimacy for church spectacle. Some very large churches emphasized connection and participation in pursuit of elusive discipleship, yet even with focus on hospitality, excellent contemporary praise bands, and digital communication, the relationship between church and people took on the attitudes and fickleness of the consumer culture. People were understood (in the church office) in terms of metrics. Butts in seats, as it were. The megachurch phenomenon—though yet alive and desired—waned (which Lyle Schaller predicted) as the boomer generation retires. Some pastors, once having an audience in the thousands, departed for opportunities that would take on a missional, smaller approach.

Though the emphasis has shifted toward mission-thinking during the first quarter of the twenty-first century, we notice the lingering presence of the attractional model, particularly as church leaders strive to re-attract participants who dropped out during the pandemic and denominational schisms. Whether it be through missional events or the normative, ordained calling to preach sermons, church culture internalizes a familiar perspective: to be a successful church, you need to have excellent content.

It is no longer surprising to see small, traditional churches utilize the strategies tested during the megachurch era. Because of unprecedented success, attractional methodology is a template. Nothing is wrong with robust sermon series, inspiring music, and rigorous hospitality. However, when the desired outcome of a cool multimedia sermon series is to enhance the brand of a church, essential connection and meaning can be hard to prove. At least we should learn to ask, no matter what the content, "By adding this function or activity, what do we lose?"

You Can't Download Belonging

Johann Sebastian Bach is appreciated as one of the most accomplished musicians of all time. Bach was also writing his music for churches. Bach probably would not have considered himself a worship pastor, but it is worth noting that Christian tradition creates some of the best music that all of culture has ever heard.

The church still seems to reach for that awareness, but it's safe to say that mass culture no longer considers the church's music the best on offer. Yet the large-church leaders focused on access to music. Some could go to a concert with a hefty ticket price, while some of us could go to a church and hear similar music with electric guitars, keyboards, multiple vocalists, and sophisticated percussion. Concerts were available every week. There were also well-produced "messages," often imitating a conference lecture or Ted Talk. Further, with adequate funding, the better the talent might be. It's no surprise that among church musicians you could also find a few atheists and lapsed Christians, because these were steady-paying gigs.

The large-church segment thrived on the fact that people had to go and physically experience the music. In rare places, a rural church could develop a phenomenal setup with enough musical talent. Or a rural congregation could call a talented speaker or teacher and keep that person long enough to create a reputation, until the pastor or leader is pulled up the ladder to a bigger and better church. Usually, rural churches couldn't compete, so it became normative for rural residents to drive up to an hour to experience the trendy suburban church with their cushioned seats and lemonade.

Now, however, internet streaming expands the range of what is accessible. To hear the best music, get on Spotify. To listen to the best speakers, download a podcast or get on YouTube. Nearly every concert, message, or talent is available to anyone, anywhere.

The emphasis on entertainment and content as the foundation of a church's presence or purpose is clashing with the connection and meaning our presence is meant to offer. It is a race against or alongside mass culture that the church can't win.

What, then, should rural churches be offering? If the content game has low odds, where should our intentions be? The answer is: exactly what the rural church has always had, particularly in a society in which our technological access leads to isolation, disconnection, and an overwhelming tsunami of choices. Our ancestors did not have our technology or luxury, but they may have had the one thing that, in the end, human beings desire more than anything else: *to belong*.

No YouTube video, podcast, or playlist can offer the core ingredients that define community. For many churches throughout history, they were constrained by inferior transportation and communication systems. How boring it must have been to show up to a place within walking distance and sit in a room with the same people you see all the time, full of basic conversations, rituals, and melodies that you can get anywhere.

How ironic it is that such mediocrity has become desirable in a society inundated with magnificence and spectacle.

The value of many churches throughout history was not their content but the belonging and meaningful connection that the content mediated. The local church offers one thing that eludes an entertainment complex or website: creating space to belong together, collectively forming together over time, and nurturing relationships that can mutually depend on one another for the benefit of the place in which they all share.

You can't download that.

Let's stop playing a game we can't win and stop focusing on an experience that fails to accomplish our purpose.

Deconstructing the Sermon

Preaching the good news is nonnegotiable, right? Well, yes, at least since the Protestant Reformation began in the sixteenth century. Many Western Christians would be perplexed by an Eastern Orthodox church service. A Quaker meeting can be unnerving for the modern evangelical Christian. Quakers sit in silence. There is no sermon. Yet, there is lots of "preaching." In some Catholic or Anglican communions, the message is simply the scripture reading for the day. Modern Christians in general might even be aghast upon witnessing an early church gathering. Where's the music? When is the sermon going to start?

Preaching can be defined as spreading the good news or proclaiming and ushering in the kingdom of God. Jesus does give a couple long sermons, yet he is constantly preaching by confronting officials, healing the sick, feeding the crowd. The good news is proclaimed even when Jesus does not use the rhetoric of a rabbinic sermon. Perhaps Jesus knows that rhetoric does not change people; experience does.

Sometimes we may presume that information is transformative. Every box of cigarettes has a warning of what will happen if you smoke. Though some teens get the warning and never start, very few people quit smoking because they read that label. Which would create more impact, Jesus giving you an inspiring talk or removing a malady that would have kept you isolated from society? Which is better, to say someone is forgiven or to watch them take up their mat and walk?

Churches face a similar problem to the warning label on a box of cigarettes. Rhetoric finds its proper place within the experience of a church culture. It's the garnish for the meal. The sermon is still useful, but it is not the only form of preaching.

Jesus is often portrayed as telling stories or having moments of interaction in response to a real context and situation. Jesus's transformative moments occur when kneeling in the sand or touching someone with an unspeakable skin disease. Most of Jesus's parables were inconclusive for his audience. Many of Jesus's defining moments used no words at all. His most catalyzing work simply dealt with asking a bunch of amateurs to follow him around for a few years and replicate what they saw.

The rural church's primary content should be an experience, one that involves real relationships in real spaces. These experiences are also void of dependence on talent, entertainment, and technological tools.

Because experiences are not downloadable.

Communicating Contextually

What does the rural church have that no one else in the region has? The answer is: your specific context and your gathered space. When content is created overtly for public consumption, the less it can reflect the context of specific people. You can listen to a Ted Talk, and it might be great information, but it cannot be crafted to the specific, phenomenological experience of a listener. Communicating with a single person allows the communicator to empathically adapt every part of their message to the receiver. It allows for feedback and direct, appropriate responses. It can take into account the setting and the environment. When done in person, there is less chance for noise: environmental disruptions or distractions.

Jesus invested heavily in a handful of individuals for three years. Those individuals took their deep formation and went on to replicate the process with another handful of disciples. Eventually, through a long process, they changed the world.

Some research suggests that the capacity limit for contextualized communication should be no larger than fifteen persons. This is group communication. Large group communication—often in the range of one hundred to two hundred people—is the approximate maximum before communication becomes generalized as public or mass communication. These limits are due to the constraints of community, because a human being is only able to know one hundred to two hundred people intimately. The average size of a rural church is thirty people. Eighty percent of UMC churches have fewer than eighty people. The largest rural church rarely exceeds two hundred people.

When preaching is done through the form of a sermon, the rural preacher is situated to speak directly to the needs, the place, the season, the situation, the time, the events, and the gifts of a unique configuration. We can know the stories sitting in the room, and we can channel what is said and what is done into what is best for the gathered group. The viability of the communication depends on how much the communicator is able to empathize with and understand their unique audience. As a result, our preaching probably won't be the most polished or the coolest, but it will be the most meaningful because there is no abstract recipient representing the general population.

Preachers in a rural context should consider spending less time on writing out their sermons. A well-crafted experience designed for the gathered community will go further than any sermon. The rhetoric is ultimately experiential in how it engages with the unique setting of the people present. Consider using less time to create the speech—"crafting a sermon"—and more time to develop the skill of extemporaneous improvisation.

By analogy, comedians put in the work to know their ideas inside and out but then are able to adapt in any given moment to the situation.

Improvisational actors train themselves to have a library of content from which they draw from, depending on what is best for their particular audience. What some consider "preaching without notes" might also be improvisational preaching. To speak extemporaneously, one feels the pulse of the people to respond with the necessary actions, communication, or moments, which will do more for a church community than a well-crafted, written sermon that takes ten, twenty, or even forty hours to write.

What Is Not Downloadable?

What other functions are not downloadable yet are highly contextualized and meaningful for a community's immediate context? Interviewing members of the community and allowing them to share their experience and story can be more effective than a monologue. Interviews also create an intimate space in which the gathered body is able to enter the narrative of someone they know and use that person's story to transform their own.

One effective form of experience in Tyler's community is called barn stations, which is a sensory experience that takes a person through a specific process. For example, every summer during the third week of July, instead of a Sunday service, the sanctuary is turned into a meditative space full of candles. A participant has a sheet—specifically written based on the situation of the community—that guides them through a mourning and grieving process. Each station has some sort of meditation and a sensory action to associate with it, to help move the information from heads to hands by engaging as many physical senses as possible. At one station, people artfully hang pictures on a board, and at the end, the community is left with a wall of saints who have recently passed, allowing participants to engage with death in a meaningful, healing way.

Michael is sometimes criticized for scribbling sermon diagrams on airplane napkins and "freestyling" the sermon as he travels across the country to seminars and events. The process still requires preparation because it comes from a decade of memorizing carefully crafted oral manuscripts.

These sermons are preached to the ear, not to the eye. Sermons never written but practiced in empty rooms or behind steering wheels.

More locally, contextual and non-downloadable preaching requires archeological spade work in one's Tel (the mound where you live). We need to excavate the signs, symbols, and stories created over centuries through the accumulation of successive layers of people inhabiting a place. This is why Jesus's parables are so specifically nuanced. He's using the framework of his location, history, and community to shape his message.

One of my first sermon series at Wildwood had a cheesy title, "The Railroad to Revival." It was a sermon series to help me make a connection with the people, and folk still remember and talk about it today. Digging into the history of the railroad and its failure, and the economic downturn it caused, was a painful point for the "wild ones." I could make a connection in my own life, growing up in the context of poverty and taking an under-the-table construction job at age fifteen. As I visited members in their homes, I inquired if they had pictures or mementos from their railroad days. In the series, I flashed up black-and-white images of parishioners and their families at work on the railroad in different capacities. I paused to ask people if they could guess who the people in the pictures were. They responded boisterously with laughter, blushing, and even applause. I connected their stories to biblical texts. But each week I framed the messages around a shared hopeful vision that our best days were yet ahead. Because God is the God of new creation, we only needed to experience a death to get to resurrection.

I can't imagine anyone wanting to download that series. Who is Ethel, and why do I care that she ran the call center? Why am I listening to a sermon about Herb the engineer? What does it matter to someone who's never heard of Wildwood that Mac and Sharon ran a diner that served guests who stopped at the station? Highly contextual preaching doesn't have broad appeal. It's very particular to a peculiar people and their place. And yet Jesus shows us the way to the universal is through the particular.

Even more resistant to downloading or repurposing are the sermonic conversations that take place in fresh expressions of church. If a sermon is an orchestra, with a conductor on a stand guiding the community through predetermined sheet music, a sermonic conversation is a jazz band. We sit down together as a community of equals, and someone strikes a note. Then each person improvises their contribution in real time. It's entirely contextual and particular to the people in that circle. What would this story look like today? What if this Jesus story is true? If it is true, how would it make a difference in my life? What is this Jesus story saying to me? People respond with personal insights, questions, and challenges. We squeeze the gospel out of the story together.

This interactive dialogue replaces the sermon hour or segment with a didactic, inquiry-based approach This is not a traditional form of proclamation, but the engagement draws immediately from collective experiences. Like Jesus, the master *teacher*, who asked more questions than he gave answers. Jesus, who rarely read manuscripts, probably never wrote one but told stories instead. These sermons are more dialogue than monologue. The purpose of any (well-conceived) sermon is to change heart and life as a response to the gospel, but these dialogical sermons also create connection and conversation and deepen relationships. You can't download that. Real conversations in real time with real people doesn't sell a brand very well, but they capture something that rhetoric, technology, and preproduced media simply cannot.

Consider other alternatives. Preaching (discipling, mentoring) could be done in micro groups of ten to fifteen people who have intimate contact on a regular basis, to be formed as followers of Jesus through those relationships (and not necessarily through explicit content). What if we put as much energy into the long process of one-on-one discipleship as we did into Sunday morning productions? Jesus already had the best process, and we've just neglected to take it seriously.

Many churches don't want children in the worship room because they are noisy and distracting, as if our children have nothing to teach us. We often claim that they need to learn how to sit quietly and listen. Perhaps we've forgotten that play and movement are the best form of learning and worship. Yet, despite the noise, the welcome presence of children in worship might relieve the anxiety of parents who do not come to gatherings for fear their children are too noisy. Some rural churches, recalling the one-room schools on the frontier, do all of children's ministry differently through an intergenerational experience. We may even find that in the intergenerational teaching of children, the adults learn more than a sermon might offer.

Think of our church gathering as a living room: a small, intimate, connected space where we sit together like an extended family. These settings are what the earliest forms of church were like. Reclaim the old ideas and transpose them to the present.

Beyond the formal content we attribute to preaching and worship, where else can a community of rural people consistently come together, connect with one another, and have shared experiences with one another? What other organization has a built-in mechanism for gathering its stakeholders once a week? Does our content and activity reflect these advantages? Do our traditional norms actually get in the way of our belonging and therefore our transformation?

The real, transformative experiences of church are not downloadable.

Field Exercise

Sermonic Conversation

First, gather your team to engage in a sermonic conversation. Chose a biblical passage and read it aloud or tell it as a story. Then ask some or all of these questions:

1. If this story happened today, what would it look like?

2. What is this story saying to me?

3. Could the story make a difference to my life? If so, how?

4. Did this story make a difference to my life? If so, how?

Using these questions as a guide, explore with the team how you might invite people to create sermonic conversations in an inquiry-based way. A practice known as *lectio devina* is a useful technique for people to relate to biblical content. As with any traditional sermon, the leader or guide for the conversation still is prepared (and has established a valued relationship) to deftly steer around the mishandling of a biblical passage as the move is made from the text to varied personal experiences.

Once you've practiced engaging with content in a new way, begin to examine all the content, events, and gathering spaces of your church. Whether it is in Sunday morning services, special events, a particular ministry, or simply the informal ways your community is in contact, ask:

1. How can we emphasize connection and relational belonging here?

2. What is in the way of a contextual focus? Are sermons written primarily for the general public? Is a food distribution failing to take into account the local needs of specific people and groups? Is an event or ministry not a reflection of what your specific area needs or has to offer? Everything from architecture, aesthetics, communication style, and the actual content itself can be considered.

3. Using the experience of relating to a particular biblical passage, how can you translate the value of those present to inform how you do everything? Quite possibly, someone's response to question two in the sermonic conversation didn't practice sound biblical exegesis. The value comes from the connection created between the people in the room and the impact a contextual moment creates for individuals. Ask, therefore, how that kind of value can become the precedent.

Field Story

Jason Villegas, Pastor, Murfreesboro UMC, Murfreesboro, North Carolina

I've served United Methodist congregations in rural eastern North Carolina for over a decade. Life has taken me across the geographical borders of different states, the theological borders of denominations, and my skin lives at the multiracial intersection of Caucasian and Latino. My mestizo, mosaic self joyfully serves in shattered, stained-glass rural church space.

When I think about rural church fresh expressions, I suggest two possibilities: One is directly connected to the institutional church, and the other is parallel but not dependent on it. I'm a "local pastor" appointed by the institutional church.

The church is a 210-year-old congregation that still bears its historic name but is no longer made up of mostly White, land-owning families. The congregation is growing again as a bilingual, multicultural group of White, Brown, and Black folk who are reconciled—more than in the sanctuary—by life around tables and in parking lots.

We define our fresh expression as the sharing of home. We are welcomed by God, who owns the earth, and from this place of welcome, we practice hospitality. God helps us share the physical space of the church buildings. We share food in bilingual meals. Our youth made a flag that mixes the Mexican, North Carolinian, and United Methodist symbols together. We continue the practice of sharing with new migrant families who come to the area for work, giving clothing, furnishings, and regular food to newcomers. Because God's gift of home is both fixed and dynamic, so is our response in living it.

Our fresh expression of church is rooted in tradition and sprouting like an old tree with new branches grafted onto it. The fruit is of a different flavor than the church was used to, but space is made for the grafting because so many branches of the old church have died. Find out what has died, name it, and grieve it. Otherwise, the people who hold power in a church may be filled with too much hidden grief to allow new grafts onto the trunk of their tradition.

Especially in rural areas, where death is so apparent, we must find ways to name the death, and then I believe we will be able to grow to see new life extending from our experiences—like a branch grafted onto a tree, like a Latino migrant welcomed home into a formerly all-White church.

CHAPTER 6

Cultivating the Kingdom of God

Place Economy

Jesus asked, "What is God's kingdom like? To what can I compare it? It's like a mustard seed that someone took and planted in a garden. It grew and developed into a tree and the birds in the sky nested in its branches." (Luke 13:18-19)

An ancient precedent for the rural church might be found in the wilderness monastic orders of early Christianity. While a central motif in several monastic communities, a phrase specific to the Rule of St. Benedict suggests some guidance for the rural church: work and pray. The monastic orders claimed that spiritual formation and reflection should be balanced by action. From their meager estates, the aesthetic monks saw prayer, liturgical worship, and meditative silence as their occupation. However, their introspection was matched by an outward pursuit of real, tactile, and beneficial service to society. Their experience of God's goodness and love led to demonstration of God's goodness and love in the world around them.

The monasteries aimed to bring life, healing, and hope to earth, economic flourishing, and the sociological structures of human communities.

Contemplation was combined with action. Their work needed formative prayer, and their prayer needed practical work.

Putting the Church in Its Proper Place

The church is more than gathering, worship, and offering services, classes, or studies. We gather to learn what it means to be disciples and thornbushes, and that leads to a responsibility to enact our discipleship. As William Temple said, "The Church is the only organization that exists for the benefit of its non-members."[1]

The primary directive is to be instruments for the building of God's kingdom. Our gatherings are where we learn how to do that: work and pray. This combination is something rural churches can enact and achieve. It's also desperately needed.

A healthy rural church will lead to healthy rural places. Rural churches can be the catalyst for realizing rural revitalization. So, how do we do this? How do we use our spiritual formation to embrace the healing of the world? How do we make God's dream real in the places we inhabit?

Un-franchising Church

What do rural places need? At the social level, the amount of addiction, hopelessness, depression, and the multitude of physical, emotional, and mental health deficits mean that our church work is more necessary than ever. The breakdown in rural families is severe. Approximately one-quarter of rural children live in single-parent homes (urban divorce rates are higher). But those living in rural areas experience a high financial and relational strain that leads to self-medication. Our communities are deteriorating, our economies are fragile, and the once-prized hallmark of food production is continually becoming more and more obsolete. The needs are there. How will our rural churches respond?

Rural churches are often viewed with stereotypical backwardness. They aren't interesting. They aren't innovative. They are, at best, quaint relics of the past and, at worst, useless. The pejorative stereotype is incorrect, but the perception feeds off the sense that something is amiss in rural churches.

The issue is rarely that a rural church doesn't do anything. In fact, in proportion to the regional population, rural churches are immensely active. The problem is that rural church leaders internalize the negative stereotypes and look for standards among the trendy, innovative ministries.

We are told that the cool, hip churches are the standard. As those churches become more notable and efficient, their processes are slowly passed down to us and, in believing that they have the answers to solve our issues, we tend to replicate what has become normal and conventional. We play the songs that are on the radio, have the equipment and media presentations that you see from the megachurches, and set up the systems, ministries, and events that worked in those places. We admire a range of suburban options and feel like we are failing unless we have those options, too.

As a result, many rural churches try to fill in a different culture's template for ministry. Where is the food bank, the prison ministry, and the men's or women's group? Where is the youth group with the traveling choir? Are we still doing VBS, card ministries, and supporting various international mission projects? Do we have a range of classes, including a DVD player, not to mention a broadband video subscription? Don't forget the ice cream social. These practices can be good, beautiful, meaningful, and transformative. The problem comes with the assumption that this is what rural churches need to do. When we are urged to fill in the blanks of a report about presumed church ministries, we are starting from the wrong place.

Place Economy

The agrarian tradition suggests a process that rural churches can consider. There was a time when rural churches and agrarianism were synchronized. In some rural places this is still understood.

Agrarianism is a way of thinking and living, based on the land, which seeks the health of the entire commonplace. Technically, agrarian thought is both political and economic because it is concerned with the whole sphere of common life, how we order our common life (politics), and how we exchange our lives, resources, and time in the places we live (economy). Agrarianism also emphasizes that the collective is best expressed through proximity. You can only care for what you can know, and you can only know what you can see. Agrarianism is the practice of living in collective cooperation with loyalty and affection for the good of a specific place that can be seen and known and cared about.

This place sounds similar to the kingdom of God. Conveniently, churches are a part of a movement with an organization that exists to foster the flourishing of the places where we dwell. Seek the shalom of the place you live; for in its shalom, you will find your shalom (Jeremiah 29:7).

"Place economy" is a phrase used in the agrarian tradition that the church ought to contemplate. Place economy is a community living in proper relation to itself; for the health of every part of itself; for the indefinite continuation of itself.

Place is an area with a common geographical proximity and a common sphere of influence. A place is where you are that can be seen, known, and cared for according to the limits of human finitude.

Economy in the agrarian perspective is how a place enacts a shared life together through the dispersal and management of resources, which includes financial and material resources but also the allocation of time, energy, labor, and attention.

This agrarian vision requires transposal. Place economy can't be franchised. It can only be meaningfully contextualized because it is dependent on the uniqueness of each place. It is the genuine and necessary response to the reality of where you are that presumes a particular loyalty and responsibility to where you belong.

With acknowledgment of rural decline, this means we have a lot of work to do. How ought we configure the work of our churches to respond to the pressing needs of our places?

The agrarian mind-set might foster food banks and prison ministries. It might generate youth groups and multimedia study groups. It could also develop grocery stores that support small, diversified farms or partner with local schools that often lack resources for programs to offer youth mentoring or family system development. It could be food production or providing access to addiction and recovery counseling. Possibly your community lacks third spaces, and you have a building with potential for gathering neighbors. Possibly there are local businesses or producers who need spaces and opportunities to grow. Do you have church property that grows grass that produces no nutrients but could be offered to 4-H groups, Future Farmers of America, or other agri-preneurs who procure access to land. Perhaps you have a platform, organizational capital, or the ability to mobilize and streamline processes and volunteers to respond to ecological, communal, or economic needs.

Place economy is a perspective that offers a different starting point for rural churches to respond to the difficult demands of their communities. This moves us closer to God's dream for the world.

Clean the local creek, throw parties, host events, offer space for town hall meetings, allow groups to hold events and retreats, organize a food cooperative, host a yoga class, or buy honey from the local beekeeper. Connect neighbors into groups who are in similar seasons of life or who share affinities, offer services like physical therapy or hairdressers or dentistry or basic medical examinations from businesses or professionals with such gifts, or promote a historical society to maintain a sense of a place's history. Find ways to support those ready to overcome addiction, and create opportunities to be and learn together that reflect the context of where you are and who you are with.

We have the opportunity to order the life of our communities in a way that reflects God's mission and Jesus's vision. Doing church differently is not only easier, but also more likely to fulfill our purpose; because catalyzing our imaginations through the lens of our places offers infinite possibilities.

When you look at your place, ask questions about how goods are produced and consumed, how the community is formed, what people are looking for, how people gather, and what they need that they either don't have or are getting in a way that doesn't align with God's good world. God chooses a very particular medium to bring about God's restoration of all things: us. The flourishing of rural places may just depend on if we are willing to accept the challenge.

Field Exercise

Holistic Health Frameworks

There are no templates for a place economy, but there are some strategic questions to consider when adapting the work to your place. In this field exercise we offer a framework for the questions that we use. Some are specifically formatted with an ecological and economic intention, but any church can think of these like keys of a song to be transposed to what makes the most sense.

Questions for individual health:

1. How do we help people live in proper relation to themselves physically, emotionally, and mentally?

2. How do we offer opportunities for people to use their unique gifts as human beings?

3. How do we offer opportunities for people to spend their time and energy in meaningful ways in comparison to our culture's current offerings?

Questions for relational health:

Now consider interpersonal relationships, neighborliness, and family systems.

4. Do people have ample opportunity to be together?

5. Do families have access to support, activities, and experiences that nurture their bonds and relieve the financial strains and busy pace of their lives?

6. Do people have access to conflict-resolution opportunities or alleviation of domestic violence and abuse?

7. Do people and neighbors feel safe to be vulnerable and share their lives together?

Questions for communal health:

8. Is there ample means to support local businesses, organizations, and administrative bodies who, in rural communities, often lack access and opportunity to meet their needs?

9. Are there members of our community who are unsupported or unprotected? How can we create equality, access, and justice through interdependence as opposed to only offering charity?

10. What gifts of our community are going unused, and what needs of our community are being unmet?

11. Is there ease of access to information and communication systems for all members of the community in regards to the community's life? Are various methods needed to make information accessible to different groups?

Questions for economic and ecological health:

12. Decentralization: Does the way we live come from our place and for the good of our place? How do we support an economy on a local, collaborative scale? Can we create a decentralized economic system by making, networking, and supporting local businesses, farmers, homesteaders, and producers?

13. Sustainability: Is everything we do able to continue indefinitely? Where sustainability has been compromised, is there a restorative approach to reverse the trend?

14. Healthy: Does our communal life embody wholeness and reflect the potential of being the best version of ourselves as human beings and in our relationships, communities, social systems, and ecosystems?

15. Intentional: Do we prioritize natural, organic, and local processes that are superior to easy, fragile craftsmanship often reflected in industrial practices? Do we value the craft of homemade over the standard of profit?

Can we develop in our area of influence a communal, health-oriented, thriving collaboration of enterprises to demonstrate alternative structures, offer healthy choices for consumption and production, and continually promote the health and culture of our places in an affordable, accessible, and inclusive way?

Do the products, goods, and services of our place reflect ecologically sound and socially conscious outcomes? Do they contribute to the health of our place? Are they primarily for our geographic proximity? Are they primarily owned and distributed locally?

Field Story

Tammy Champagne, Laity, Sparr, Florida: population unknown

Our pastor, Stacey, encouraged me to go to a Fresh Expressions training, and I agreed because of a free lunch. The free lunch led to a dinner church, Lakes and Meadows, which, as of this story, is three years old.

We are a rural dinner church in Marion County, Florida. The Lakes and Meadows community is located in a very rural area, and its residents are elderly, disabled, alcoholics, addicts, criminals, generational welfare families, and farmers. The first thing we learned is that our area is not like the inner-city, urban areas discussed at the training. Therefore, we adapted menus and how we approach people with a new faith practice, and we devoted many hours building relationships with the community. In sum, we created, adapted, changed, and morphed into a church that has grown organically out of its community. The lives of our people may still be hard and unfair, but today they have a better understanding of what it means to have the church stand with them.

We began by serving food, loving the people, and sharing Jesus stories to a crowd of fifteen (mostly our volunteers). Over three years Lakes and Meadows attracted three traditional rural churches to be Christ to this community and invited them to be Christ with us. We now serve food to over sixty people every Monday night. But more important, we pray with them, we know their stories, they are a part of us, we are a part of them, and we are all a part of God.

Sometimes we make church too hard. It's really easy to gather church if we do it in a different way—the rural way!

CHAPTER 7

Field Cred

Key Ingredients to Rural Church Leadership

But you are a chosen race, a royal priesthood, a holy nation,
a people who are God's own possession. You have become this people
so that you may speak of the wonderful acts of the one who called you
out of darkness into his amazing light. (1 Peter 2:9)

Perhaps you've heard of "street cred," which is the acceptance and respect that's earned by someone's commitment to a particular location.
One is said to have "street cred" if that person survived and thrived in the
shared circumstances of a neighborhood. Street cred is also attributed to
those who are practitioners of their subject matter. Our people care very
little about our graduate degrees. They are more concerned that we show up,
be present, and roll up our sleeves when there's work to be done.

So, we want to tell you about "field cred," the acceptance and respect
that's earned by someone's commitment to a particular flourishing rural
context. We've collected the diverse stories of leaders from a diversity of
rural contexts. These people have legitimate credibility in rural ministry
because they live it every day.

What can we learn about leadership from practitioners of rural ministry across the United States? First, we acknowledge there are not "seven

simple steps to successful rural church leadership." No one size fits all. We find it a better investment to visit rural leaders and shadow them for a day, to see their place and watch how they interact within it.

Christian leadership starts with a deep commitment to following Jesus. Faithfulness must precede fruitfulness. In Jesus, he is the vine, we are the branches, and fruit is the result of remaining in relationship, and not necessarily effort on our part (John 15:1-11). In Jesus's way of leadership, the greatest are the least, and the strongest are the meek. To be a leader in the way of Jesus is to wash feet (John 13:14).

The foundation of leadership in the rural context is *trust*. You can have great ideas, and you can have wondrous mobilization efforts for teams, but you are dealing with people. Even in lateral leadership, if the people you are working with do not trust you, then none of it will work.

To establish trust, you have to care. This empathy is not particular to rural places, but it is a heightened expectation. Our communities don't invest their time, energy, and resources in ideas or experiences or concepts. They invest those precious gifts in relationships. It sounds obvious, but relational leadership requires that there is a relationship.

The first suggestion we would offer to any rural church leader—clergy or lay—is to put your telescope down and root your feet where you are. Listen. Pay attention. Care.

Before you can lead, you must belong. Before you can belong, you must be known. And to be known, you must be present in real relationships with real people whom you genuinely care about. Sometimes that requires getting out of the way. Sometimes that means stepping aside from platform or desire to cast vision. Just listen.

There are some other key ingredients to rural church leadership that seem to recur across a multitude of contexts. Rural leadership, like a Cajun recipe, has certain ingredients that must be included. As practitioners of rural ministry, we think some particular ingredients are helpful. We suggest it's time to rethink and redeploy the circuit rider.

Bring Back the Circuit Riders

In a post-Christendom society, many rural church buildings sit empty. An institutional system that was already backward and failing has been more fully exposed by the emergence of COVID-19. Yet some rural pioneers have continued to engage in fruitful ministry. Others have focused on forming new Christian communities out in the first, second, and third places of the larger context, with people who don't go to church. This activity often leads to the renewal of the existing congregations, a phenomenon we call "re-missioning." It's based in bringing new life to congregations from the outside in, rather than internal tinkering.[1]

It's time to rethink the idea of itinerant clergy serving rural circuits. Rather than understanding itinerancy in the institutional sense of being sent annually from one local church to another, we would recover the apostolic genius of the circuit rider. Local clergy now find ourselves in communities where we need to be both missionaries and pastors. New strange kinds of circuits are emerging, consisting of traditional congregations and fresh expressions that form in analog and digital spaces. Itinerancy, in its contemporary manifestation, might be less about traveling to different spaces and more about traveling around your current space differently.

On Sunday mornings, co-pastors Jill and Michael join their team for the 9:00 a.m. worship experience at Wildwood UMC. Every aspect of the service, including the preaching, is carried out by teams of lay leaders in a co-creative and shared leadership approach. We then drive the thirty minutes to Ocala, where the 11:00 a.m. worship experience of St Mark's takes place in the same way, as teams of laity work together. While this is happening, another team of laypersons distributed across multiple states are conducting online worship experiences in a 1,400-member community called Living Room Church. Throughout the seven-day week, both pastors and laypersons are offering digital worship experiences, devotionals, prayer times, yoga church, tattoo talks, and spiritual conversations. A daily study through the whole Bible called the "Daily Dose" is led by Adam Fike, a lay minister!

The trend will continue with fewer full-time "professional ministers" and more bi-vocational and co-vocational missionary-pastors. The future of the church, rural or otherwise, is simple, lay-led, and low cost. In this new space, we need a fresh take on a vintage tradition of the minister as "circuit rider," and it is a true "priesthood of all believers."[2]

ReThinking Leadership

Earlier, we reimagined the parish (a region or area serving as the mission field of a church, priest, or pastor). Now let's explore what remixing leadership for a new generation of circuit riders looks like. Specifically, we'll dive into shared, relational, and decentralized forms of leadership. We'll begin here with *shared*.

More leaders are exhausted, burned out, and quitting the ministry than ever before. Much of this comes down to our concept and practice of leadership. Jill and Michael Beck often jest that we are the co-pastors of a fifteen-point charge! We serve two inherited traditional congregations, and alongside those we oversee over a dozen fresh expressions of church. Obviously, a traditional, hierarchal leadership would not work well in this scenario. If we take a page from the early circuit riders, we could perhaps learn some principles that can be contextualized for a new missional frontier.

Those early circuit riders had to be young, in good health (when they started), and single (the rigors of traveling ministry were too difficult for families).[3] Early Methodist circuit riders did not have a formal education and often had no ecclesiastical credentials. Circuit riders often moved to a new circuit every year. Being moved to a new area gave the preachers an opportunity to reuse and perfect their sermons. This meant the people of the fledgling congregations took responsibility for the ministry. It also safeguarded the congregations from forming a dependent relationship with their assigned minister and falling into a state of learned helplessness.

We think rural ministry requires permeance, a deep commitment to a place, but our place is an interior circuit. The whole area is our parish. Every space is a place where church can form. And every person is a potential missionary.

Circuit riders, traveling great distances across the frontier and overseeing multiple communities, had to employ a leadership strategy that was shared, relational, and decentralized. Their approach has implications for rural ministry today.

Two Distinct Leadership Styles

Perhaps a fitting way to describe shared leadership is to contrast it with its counterpart, positional leadership. Two biblical examples, Abimelech and Tola, form the analogy. In contrast to Abimelech's three-year reign of terror that preceded him (to which is devoted an entire chapter in Judges 9), the Bible devotes merely two short verses to the twenty-three-year reign of Tola: "After Abimelech, Tola son of Puah and grandson of Dodo, a man of Issachar, arose to rescue Israel. He lived in Shamir in the Ephraim highlands. For twenty-three years he led Israel; then he died and was buried in Shamir" (Judges 10:1-2).

Chieftain Abimelech was a complete disaster of a leader, narcissistic, self-serving, and brutal in his pursuit of and consolidation of power. Tola "rose to deliver Israel" and humbly, quietly, and wisely ruled for over two decades. Tola didn't make headlines. The Bible records no controversy. We imagine the two leaders embody two types of leadership:

Positional/hierarchal individualistic approach (Abimelech)
Shared/adaptive collectivistic approach (Tola)

The nineteenth-century Ukrainian rabbi and biblical scholar Malbim highlights the distinction between the two in this way, "Abimelech sought to lord it over the Israelites as his subjects, whereas Tola sought to help them and take care of their needs."[4]

Positional leaders are often more focused on authority, executing responsibilities, problem/solution thinking, and safeguarding their position from organizational politics and challenges. They generally operate on the organization through their positional power.

Shared, lateral leadership isn't glamorous, though. You don't get to be the rock star or the hero.

Trinity as a Paradigm

The Trinity is a paradigm for shared leadership. Who is the leader in the triune God? The dynamic relational nature of the Creator, Redeemer, and Sustainer contrasts starkly with the static hierarchies we so often see embedded in the church. In the triune God, we see a dynamic, relational movement and dance of leadership. The Trinity is not a hierarchy, with one person in authority over the other persons, but an interactive, nonlinear, relational community.

Perichoresis, the relational dance of mutual indwelling, is not about one person of the Trinity ruling over the others. It is a shared mode, each making room for the other, each taking the lead of the divine dance at different times.

At Pentecost, the "power" Jesus promised (Acts 1:8) was poured out in a shared, adaptive, and collectivistic way. The power was distributed throughout the entire community. All of the disciples were empowered and gifted as a community of equals, with a clear missional focus (Acts 2:4). The "power" was shared, relational, decentralized, and self-organized. This enabled the disciples to spread the love of Jesus from "Jerusalem, in all Judea and Samaria, and to the end of the earth" (Acts 1:8). Jesus's ascension is not just about where Jesus goes; it is also about where Jesus leaves. For the disciples to be Jesus's body on earth, Jesus's physical presence had to leave to make room for the disciples to carry the work forward. Jesus is telling the disciples, "You're going to have to do this." And he isn't being lazy. It's good leadership. Because the God's kingdom everybody. Jesus leads by letting go, empowering, and making room so the work can be shared.

Recovery Fellowships

One movement that embodies shared leadership is the twelve-step recovery group. The "second tradition" of these communities expresses the essence of shared leadership, "For our group purpose there is but one ultimate authority—a loving God as experienced in our group conscience. Our leaders are but trusted servants; they do not govern."[5]

Since their founding in 1935, and with hundreds of thousands of groups across the world, recovery fellowships have not been scandalized by abuses of power.

While there is still a place and need for positional leadership, positional authority is an ineffective default in the rural context. The most thriving rural shepherds lead from relationships.

Shared Leadership

An argument broke out among the disciples over which one of them should be regarded as the greatest. But Jesus said to them,

> The kings of the Gentiles rule over their subjects, and those in authority over them are called 'friends of the people.' But that's not the way it will be with you. Instead, the greatest among you must become like a person of lower status and the leader like a servant. So which one is greater, the one who is seated at the table or the one who serves at the table? Isn't it the one who is seated at the table? But I am among you as one who serves. (Luke 22:24-27)

One mistake clergy make in a rural context is rushing in to "fix the problems" of the community with the attitudes of positional leadership. We see ourselves as the solution, the heroic solo leader who will save the day. We begin doing the "work of ministry" to and for the people. In some cases, this can lead to a revitalization (if we don't burn out in the process). What we actually do is make ourselves indispensable. The church is oriented around us and our gifts. If we leave, the work collapses.

I (Michael) know this syndrome from my own track record of failures. Each of the revitalizations I led early in my ministry collapsed as soon as I left. Additionally, I burned out several times in the process.

Leadership is more sustainable when energizing a community of people toward accomplishing a shared mission. This kind of leadership is actually followership, because following Jesus well is the source of Christlike leadership. There is only one Messiah, and a church body has only one head. The focus shifts from the action of the "leader" to the many members of the body who are in the community. The community must internalize their own challenges and discover their own inner resources to meet those challenges.

The mission is the relationships. The relationships are the mission. From those relationships, clergy can empower the whole people of God.

Team-Based Ministry

God has given his grace to each one of us measured out by the gift that is given by Christ. That's why scripture says, *When he climbed up to the heights, he captured prisoners, and he gave gifts to people.*

What does the phrase "he climbed up" mean if it doesn't mean that he had first gone down into the lower regions, the earth? The one who went down is the same one who climbed up above all the heavens so that he might fill everything.

He gave some apostles, some prophets, some evangelists, and some pastors and teachers. His purpose was to equip God's people for the work of serving and building up the body of Christ until we all reach the unity of faith and knowledge of God's Son. God's goal is for us to become mature adults—to be fully grown, measured by the standard of the fullness of Christ. (Ephesians 4:7-13)

Moses' father-in-law said to him, "What you are doing isn't good. You will end up totally wearing yourself out, both you and these people who are with you. The work is too difficult for you. You can't do it alone." (Exodus 18:17-18)

Shared leadership requires a *team-based approach* and ultimately releases a *priesthood of all believers*. Here I (Michael) unpack what a "team-based approach" looks like in my context.

Jill Beck and I serve together with a team of dedicated lay leaders, whom we call "pastors" in our context. We serve together as a pastoral team. Jill and I are each appointed one-quarter of our time to the congregations. In theory this translates to ten hours weekly; in practice we all know the well-worn cliché that "there's no such thing as a part time pastor!" This *team-based appointment* approach is rare (at present) for a small congregation struggling to survive month by month.

Each person on the team brings a specific set of gifts to the team. Some, being more gifted with caring and shepherding, have a passion to nurture people into the fullness of who they are in Christ. Jill, while also having those caring, pastoral tendencies, is gifted in organization and administration with a tilt toward the prophetic. My gifts are missional and evangelistic, with a strong tendency to teach (cf. Ephesians 4:11).

Each of us also brings a different leadership impulse to the table:

Relational Leadership: Concerns attention and activity patterns that discover, initiate, nurture, and sanction the human connections that compose a social entity.

Implemental Leadership: Concerns the implementation of a set of competencies and skills for experiments, systems, and practices by which we live out our identity and agency.

Adaptive Leadership: Concerns an innate ability to adapt to diverse, chaotic, and complex environments, thereby assisting organizations and individuals in dealing with consequential changes in uncertain times, when no clear answers are forthcoming.

We pursue a shared leadership approach. We seek to embody the perichoretic nature of the Trinity, a circle dance, where each of us shares in taking the lead at different times in the song. We invite the congregation and people from the larger community into that circle dance.

None assume we have all the answers. None see ourselves as the hero who will come in and carry the congregation on our backs toward revitalization. We know the solution to the congregation's problems is within ourselves. Our role is to help discover together the inner resources the Spirit has already provided for our own transformation.

Now you may be saying to yourself, "This kind of leadership won't apply to my context! I have *no* staff, much less a team!" I hear your concern. I have never been appointed full time to a single church in my entire ministry. I have never had a full-time staff person. At churches I served previously, I was the *only* staff person, and *very* part time at that. Yet at each of those places, the "team" started with a handful of faithful laity who had shining eyes. You don't need staff to have a team. In fact, we think the idea of paid Christians receiving full salaries to do the work of the church is a remnant of Christendom. We don't think that's actually what Jesus intended when he sent the disciples forth, two by two.

This approach to shared leadership might be received with hope in the rural contexts that cannot afford full-time paid leadership. But we believe it won't be long before the model is necessary for revitalization and multiplication in any place.

At our parish of circuits, we organize team-based ministry in every area:

- A core team meets weekly to make decisions democratically for the church.

- Teams work together to provide pastoral care.

- A team of preachers, consisting of both lay and clergy, organize and provide the preaching ministry of the church.

- Teams organize and carry out the drive-through community dinners.

- Teams set up for and conduct worship.

- Teams from different groups work together on outreach and recovery ministries.

- Teams cultivate fresh expressions of church together.

- Teams handle the digital aspects of the ministry, website, social media, streaming, and so on.

Priesthood of All Believers

But you are a chosen race, a royal priesthood, a holy nation, a people who are God's own possession. You have become this people so that you may speak of the wonderful acts of the one who called you out of darkness into his amazing light. (1 Peter 2:9)

Martin Luther wrote, "a priest, especially in the New Testament, was not made but was born. He was created, not ordained. He was born not indeed of flesh, but through a birth of the Spirit, by water and the Spirit in the washing of regeneration (John 3:6f.; Titus 3:5f.). Indeed, all Christians are priests and all priests are Christian." Luther went on to convey the sacredness of all work: "Every occupation has its own honor before God. Ordinary work is a divine vocation or calling. In our daily work, no matter how important or mundane, we serve God by serving the neighbor, and we also participate in God's on-going providence for the human race."[6]

Aside from the well-known accusations of "enthusiasm," a focus on personal testimonies of conversion, and the boisterous nature of the early "shouting Methodists," John Wesley assembled, trained, deployed, and oversaw a small army of lay preachers—the whole people of God. Asbury took the seeds of these revolutionary ideas even further.

One of the major shifts enabled by digital technology is the "gig economy," which is a labor market characterized by short-term contracts or freelance work rather than permanent jobs.

In a gig labor force, participants work multiple jobs and side hustles and generate multiple income streams. Because the twentieth-century model for professional leadership with a pension is no longer sustainable in declining communities, Christian leaders are not exempt from the temporizing forces in gig economics. Many retiring clergy cannot afford to retire from "full time ministry," and we expect the trend to escalate.[7] In the future, there will be more and more co-vocational and bi-vocational clergy—tentmakers like Paul the Apostle (Acts 18:1-4).

In rural ministry, we do get a part-time check from a congregation, but we also have several other sources of part-time employment. Many pastors serving rural appointments probably tithe more to their church than they get paid. Jill and Michael joke that they have five other "full-time jobs" for part-time pay.

There are advantages. The expectations of sitting in an office, making every hospital call, doing every home visit, are reconsidered. *The only way the ministry can go forward is in a strategically team-based, every-person-a-priest kind of way.* The expectation at our congregations is that we together are a *priesthood of all believers*. We share the work of ministry. And we share in the joy of the harvest together.

If you're an entrepreneur, the gig approach is a freedom scenario for starting a business in the community, getting a local part-time job through which you can connect with people in the community, teaching at the local school or college, or commuting to work in a nearby town. These are all life-giving possibilities, which when intentional can bear missional fruit for the congregation.

With the mind-set of the "priesthood of all believers," *the whole church restructures itself to focus half our energy on caring for the congregation and half our energy planting fresh expressions in the community.*

Renegotiating the Social Contract

For the gig-based rural ministry to work, a renegotiation of the social contract is required. The current social contract between pastors and congregations is based in part on bureaucratic procedures in the institutional forms of the denominational franchise economy.

In the franchise church, the pastor is producer of religious goods and services, and the people are customers with need to consume those goods. In this setting, it can be much harder for laity to find a missional avenue for self-expression.

In an *every-person-a-priest* approach to ministry, coupled with part-time gig-pastors and staff, there might not be a pastor-appreciation month, and there are rarely raises, Christmas bonuses, or paid vacation.

There is also a potential compromise that our ministries, content, and "productions" will be less than ideal or "excellent." But the meaning is in the mess. Real is not always glamorous, but it is always beautiful.

The shared, relational, decentralized, self-organizing approach to leadership is recommended for churches wanting to reimagine their existence in the places they minister. These concepts of leadership can be difficult to demonstrate, partly because they are countercultural and partly because they are dependent on other people. Sometimes it is easier to do the work yourself. We avoid the drama, we retain control, and we don't need to count on others. This myopic perspective is easier in the short-term, but it's unsustainable.

Shared rural leadership plays the long game, which is also a new mind-set for congregations that learned to hibernate during the current appointment in case the next pastor is better.

Field Exercise

Leadership Self-Evaluation

If you embrace these ideas of shared leadership, team-based ministry, and a priesthood of all believers, start with some questions to address in introspective prayer with God.

1. Am I willing to grow fruit on other peoples' trees rather than my own? Am I willing to equip, empower, and celebrate others, rather than be the center of celebration?

2. Fruitful rural ministry is not the result of one overnight gig. It takes years. Am I willing to give years of my life to these people and this community?

3. Do I genuinely love these people? Do I love this place? Do I feel God calling me to this work?

4. Do I weep over this zip code? Does my heart break for the things that break God's heart here? Do I see the fragmentation, and am I willing to give my life serving in the gaps?

5. Where do I need to listen more and speak less? How can I weave into the fabric of the people I am with?

6. When I do speak, cast vision, imagine a new thing, or compel the community, am I doing this with them or to them?

If you can answer these questions in the affirmative and be self-aware of your presence and disposition, your calling may fit with rural church leadership.

Field Story

Stacey Spence, Elder, Three-point Charge, Sparr, Pine, and Hawthorne, Florida

I once told my mother I hoped God would use me in ministry and combine that ministry with horses. My mom said, in a loving and kind way, "Good luck with that."

I've always been an equestrian, but I never realized how horses and God could work together for the betterment of society. I started as a volunteer for Stirrups and Strides (SnS), which is a therapeutic riding center, teaching abled-differently people how to ride, compete in shows, and connect with creation. Specifically, for therapeutic help with spinal trauma, autism, Down syndrome, and more. When I saw how the connection between the horse and participant healed and strengthened the body and mind of the participant, I was hooked.

While I was in seminary and working at SnS, people would come to me for prayer, advice, and encouragement. Children who would be distracted in church service found a way to be connected to faith through our work at SnS. When a volunteer would pass away, I was asked to do the funerals. We began to incorporate meditation into riding lessons, and I became the chaplain for the farm. Currently at SnS, I work with veterans (active and retired, men and women) who are in a rehabilitation program, using faith and fun with horses to heal the broken nature of life.

In the rural setting of a farm, with horse, dog, and cat, we've tapped the teachings of Jesus and the writings of Richard Rohr, Thomas Merton, and Leonard Sweet, and we've made the table a focus of our connection. This ministry brings all walks of life together. Most riders have a scholarship, and often this is the only exercise our students receive throughout the week. In this setting, faith is mentioned and prayers are not offered constantly.

This work with differently abled people has also had a direct effect on how the church behaves. Most established churches do not offer an environment comfortable for abled-differently people. Because we are learning how "different" people process their faith, traditional churches are finding new ways of encountering difference in the culture.

In this equestrian expression of ministry, we don't have a formal worship time or church service, but we do mutually encounter the love of Christ, which is offered to every person who enters the farm.

CHAPTER 8

Somewhereness and Somebodiness

The Lord said to him, "What's that in your hand?" (Exodus 4:2)

So what should a rural church look like? Start with somewhereness and somebodiness.

Somewhereness

Somewhereness is another way to talk about place economy. It's about loving the creation of which we are inextricably bound, including every little cell that makes up every lily and every person.

To understand somewhereness, the French word *terroir* is helpful. Every place has a unique flavor or a distinct taste. The *terroir* (French—from medieval Latin *territorium*) refers to the totality of tones, textures, and tastes. Every context has a unique one-of-a-kind flavor and a unique set of ingredients to compose that flavor into its best possible realization. *Terroir* refers to a *somewhereness*.

Think of how the natural environment of a grapevine influences what kind of wine is produced. Cumulative factors such as soil, topography, and climate contribute to the *terroir*. The characteristics of a wine's taste are a result of the contextual factors involved in its growth and production. When wine or coffee has a distinct flavor or scent, your gustatory and olfactory senses are discerning the *terroir*—the somewhereness.

Terroir must be experienced. You can't read about environmental factors to taste somewhereness. You have to be vulnerable. You raise your hand to the most vulnerable place on your body: your face. You take a risk; you let it wash over your tongue; you digest it. It becomes part of you. If it's spoiled, it can make you sick. If it's whole, it can awaken and lubricate your consciousness, or even impair it. The *terroir* of your context cannot be experienced by reading statistical reports or asking others to measure it. You immerse yourself in the context in order to taste the somewhereness for yourself.

What is the somewhereness of your community? What are the key factors that make it what it is? Where did it come from? Where is it now? What's life-giving about your somewhere? Where are the sore spots that need healing? Where is it heading in its current trajectory? Where is cosmic collision with the new creation breaking into your place? Where are some serious course corrections needed?

The fresh-expressions way is about cultivating communities of the kingdom in the everyday rhythms and spaces where people already do life. Christian community is forming at the barn, bar, lakeside, local diner, farmers market, and so on. But it's also forming in telephone conferences, Zoom rooms, and virtual-reality headsets.

We call this a blended ecology of church, and its power lies in how the church's life can spread out across the whole ecosystem. Teams go into these various spaces, following the listening, loving, building relationships, sharing Jesus, church, repeat, journey we discussed earlier. This activity cultivates little islands of new creation dotting the landscape. Every space in the community is a potential habitat of the Spirit, and every person plays a role. This helps us restore a sense of somewhereness to our parish.

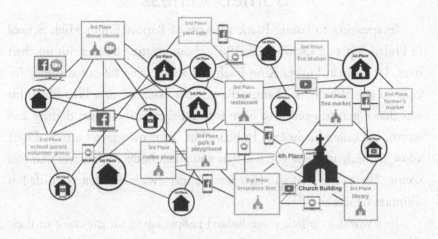

The groups that form in these spaces can be centered around all kinds of common interests and hobbies. Christian community can form around social justice, food production, or creation care. Christians and non-Christians can work together for the betterment of the whole parish in centered-set forms of community. Whereas bounded-set communities typically have a clearly defined boundary, like a fence, requiring the right gate code to get in, centered-set communities have a clearly defined center, a common goal, a shared passion, or a person—in our case, Jesus. People can be at various levels of relationship to the center, moving away or moving closer, but all are welcome to explore in some capacity.

Somewhereness, a missional posture of placefulness, is essential to begin healing a sick mother of a planet. It's essential to see how the kingdom of God is growing subversively all through our parish like a mustard seed (Luke 13:18-21). It puts us in proximity to our neighbor, where we can seek the good of our place and learn to love those we share our place with more fully. Which means somewhereness must always include somebodiness.

Somebodiness

In speaking to young Black students at Barratt Junior High School in Philadelphia on October 26, 1967, about creating a blueprint for their lives, Dr. Martin Luther King Jr. shared about what he called the "principle of somebodiness." King believed that essential to a life's blueprint was that a person needed to have a deep belief in their own dignity and worth. He called his hearers to believe in "your own *somebodiness*. Don't allow anybody to make you feel that you are nobody. Always feel that you count. Always feel that you have worth, and always feel that your life has ultimate significance."[1]

In a world in which some judged people based on the color of their skin rather than the content of their character, King was teaching these young people that they were beautiful, that they mattered, that they were created in the image of God. He was shaping these young minds to see themselves as persons of sacred worth and infinite value.

In Jesus's teaching to love our neighbor as ourselves, the implicit assumption is that we will have a healthy sense of self-love. If we love ourselves badly, we will most likely love our neighbor badly as well. Or as we say in the recovery fellowships, "you can't give what you don't have."

Growing in our love for God instills a divine sense of somebodiness. But we can't stop there. We must extend that same somebodiness to every person we encounter. *Ubuntu*: We are persons through other persons.

Somebodiness is loving our neighbor until it's enough; in other words, indefinitely.

In the soil map preface to this book, we recalled that Francis Asbury wasn't alone in his work of barnstorming the backcountry. The story of Asbury, the founding bishop of American Methodism, shouldn't be told apart from Harry Hosier, the founding evangelist of American Methodism. Harry Hosier—also known as "Black Harry"[2]—was a freed slave, illiterate, never formally ordained, and yet was known as the greatest orator in America.[3] In many cases, Hosier was the first Black preacher that White crowds had ever heard.[4]

Hosier began traveling with Asbury sometime between 1775 and 1780, first as a traveling companion and assistant. But it didn't take long for Hosier to prove himself as an equal and colleague. Typically, Asbury would preach to the White people, and Hosier focused on persons experiencing slavery, but this evolved over time. Hosier would step in for Asbury when he was sick but was often asked to preach immediately following Asbury.[5]

People asked to hear Hosier, and Asbury admitted that the best way to draw a large crowd was to announce that Hosier would preach. Hosier's style was emotional and compelling. He connected deeply with the hopes and fears of common people and could memorize passages of Scripture and songs that he heard: "Hosier relied on his memory and imagination to produce flowery figures of speech and delivered them with an impressive voice and bold gestures.[6]

Bishop Thomas Coke traveled with Hosier during one of his visits and said of him, "I really believe he is one of the best Preachers in the world, there is such an amazing power that attends his preaching, though he cannot read; and he is one of the humblest creatures I ever saw."[7] His preaching helped the Methodists become the most prominent denomination in the country.

Asbury and Hosier, like a dynamic duo, traveled hundreds of thousands of miles and preached tens of thousands of sermons throughout the vast expanses of a fledgling nation. While Asbury seemed to have the genius for organization, it was to Hosier whom people thronged to hear his spellbinding sermons.

Stephen Webb makes a compelling case for connecting Indiana University's namesake "Hoosiers" back to its forgotten origin. Over time *Hoosier* was a common synonym for a yokel or bumpkin. But like the term *Methodist*, which was once derogatory and aimed to insult, the term *Hoosier* was used as a badge of pride by Indiana citizens. The origins trace back to the racist idea that Methodists were so uneducated and simple they would follow a Black minister. As waves of Methodists settled in Indiana, they carried the term Hoosier with them. Webb argues that over time the racial connotations were gradually stripped away and lost to history.[8]

Webb noted that Hosier "dramatized Biblical stories in order to impress upon his listeners the urgency of God's offer of salvation."[9] Hosier was a pioneer of preaching non-downloadable content. Beginning in 1789, Hosier also traveled with Freeborn Garrettson, the ardent emancipationist. Garrettson would often leave the preaching to Hosier, as he tended to other matters.[10]

Unfortunately, Hosier was both an outsider and an insider to the movement he helped flourish. Because of his race, he was kept on the periphery of leadership. As American Methodism began the process of building institutions, it reverted to (and split over) racist tendencies. Methodists gained respectability and emphasized formal education and ordination. Ordination was not equally granted to Blacks. For a further example, as open-air gatherings moved more and more into constructed buildings, Blacks were forced into segregated seating arrangements. At the outdoor campmeetings, people of different races could sit together, but inside it was considered inappropriate.[11] One of us served a congregation in which the converted "negro seating" area was still a feature of the sanctuary.

Blacks once welcomed as equals in the Methodist movement, were now forced to defend their sense of somebodiness. They had to make a decision to stay in those racist conditions or start their own churches. Hosier is sometimes contrasted with Richard Allen (1760–1831), the founding Bishop of what became the African Methodist Episcopal Church (AME). The two attended the Christmas Conference at Lovely Lane Chapel that began December 24, 1784, in which a new Methodist Episcopal Church was founded. They were the only two Black persons in attendance, but it is unknown whether they knew each other personally.

Much of American Methodist's early growth came from Black churches. From 1790 to 1810, one fifth of Methodist membership was comprised of African Americans.[12] Yet as many people who rallied to hear

"Black Harry" preach with uncanny and even supernatural eloquence and power, many more found the integration of Whites and Blacks profoundly disturbing. Webb argues it was during this time period that the derogatory term *Hoosier* came into common use: "His congregations were rural and unsophisticated, and they mixed the races, two characteristics that would have prompted hostility and ridicule."[13]

American Methodists' passion for abolition was born from real relationships with Black persons, who worshipped and served together. It was a movement that believed in the power of somebodiness.

At the Christmas Conference, a detailed plan was approved to rid the church of slaveholders entirely. From the publication of the *Discipline* in 1785, Methodist slaveholders had twelve months to execute a legal deed of emancipation. Members who refused were to be expelled. Asbury, Coke, and a coalition of abolitionists created a petition calling for "the immediate or Gradual Extirpation of Slavery" and even met with President Washington for its endorsement. Tragically, the petition backfired, eliciting pro-slavery counterpetitions and an attempted repeal of the 1782 manumission act.[14]

As Hatch points out, the early insurgent Christians movements imparted to ordinary people, especially those experiencing poverty and marginalization, a "sense of somebodiness." As people experienced consolation in a Methodist worship service, held in a log cabin or brush arbor, they were transported into a community of belonging. As one early participant described, "an abiding confidence that he was a subject of that powerful kingdom whose Prince cared for his subjects."[15]

These gatherings are analogous to the belonging that rural places and people seek from "circles that heal." They had the essential ingredients of a healing community: they were accessible, safe, and real. The gatherings were accessible in that they took place right where people lived, in their homes, fields, and barns. They spoke a common and shared language that everyone could understand. They were safe in that all people were welcome to join and free to participate as equals. One is not a pauper, an illiterate, or a slave in this space. You are a somebody. They were real in that an honest confession of sin and testimonies of grace were welcome. People brought their real problems and found real healing.

When we try to deny the somebodiness of another person, it not only denies healing but also causes harm. Rural congregations often sit in a place where a shared history of harm is swept under the rug. In many rural locations, a Black church and a White church can be a stone's throw away. 11:00 a.m. on a Sunday continues to be the most segregated hour. Some rural communities are also highly populated by a single race or a single political party, an astonishing development as African Americans—who were mostly rural—migrated to urban centers during the growth of industrialization. Often, this was a forced migration. Even an exile.

In frontier Methodism, the campmeetings were places that broke down the repressive social structures. They were thin places, where men, women, and children, of every race and class, came together as equal somebodies, a transcendent embodiment of the gracious gift of life. These radically democratized gatherings challenged the dominating narratives of society. Over time, the gatherings were domesticated, and respectable Christianity enforced the death-dealing stereotypes about race.

Rural fresh expressions can be a new expression of those early campmeetings. It's very difficult to challenge racist, sexist, and classist structures that can find safe harbor in rural congregations. In some cases, trying to change that culture from the inside will require a miracle, not that God is beyond that sort of thing.

Here we can take from the playbook of the early insurgent forms of Christianity that gave birth and shape to the United States. We have discovered that creating new forms of community alongside existing ones can lead to a transformation of the whole ecosystem. Over time, as those communities live together in a symbiotic relationship, the dark and long-standing "isms" of congregations can be healed.

The rural church can be a significant change agent in this way. In the wilderness, we are uniquely positioned to create alternate forms of community that can heal the world. These are nascent communities where a sense of somebodiness can be equally shared among all people and where a diverse body of people can be united by their common humanity.

This transformation is possible not only regarding racism but also in the context of political extremism, prison reform, economic disadvantages, pollution, or climate change. These communities can form and exist alongside existing congregations and over time. The healing they create floods into the larger community and can even seep through the stained-glass windows of our congregations.

Tex Sample documented with research the features common to many rural contexts. Economically depressed rural communities exist at the margins of a post-industrial, globalized world and are bound together by a shared morality. This morality is a set of shared cultural norms and belief systems grounded in a community's unique history and customs. In these communities, tradition is a central force to endorse new practices, new family realities, new definitions of success, emerging values, and some vision of the American Dream. There is an enduring belief in the righteousness of the family and a commitment to a pride of place.[16]

These are good values when they bend toward justice. These are kingdom values, when they make room for all people to experience a sense of somebodiness. This is why excavating the layers of stories of our Tel is so vital.

Katherine Cramer conducted research in rural Wisconsin in which she examined "rural consciousness," the lens through which rural people view the world. She discovered that this consciousness played a significant role in terms of how people make sense of public affairs and understand politics. Cramer describes three key components of rural consciousness:

1. A perception that rural areas do not receive their fair share of decision-making power.

127

2. They see themselves as distinctly different from those who live in urban and suburban areas, and these differences are not respected by urbanites.

3. They do not receive their fair share of public resources for which they pay taxes.[17] While this is a limited sample in one state, we find some version of this rural consciousness prevalent in many rural contexts.

Yet the church, one of the few permanent stakeholders in most rural communities, can be a place where people of different cultures and with different resources, can come together to catalyze significant change. A rural congregation can be the locus of God's kingdom, a transforming instrument in the healing of the world.

Perhaps the true crisis of rural congregations is an identity crisis. Perhaps we have forgotten who we are and what a gift the rural church actually is to the world. Maybe we need to recover an insurgent form of Christianity.

We think the final form of somebodiness is the identity the rural church needs to claim itself. In a world that sees rural communities as the nobodies from nowhere, the forgotten, and the wild ones, we need to reclaim the significance of our identity—our God-given identity as God's beloved people and place. We are beloved and precious in the sight of God. Before anything else, we are somebodies from somewhere.

It's unlikely that rescue from congregational death will come about in a boardroom or get planned from the institutional center. We cannot expect our systems to come and fix the specific adaptive challenges of our particular context. Systems are not designed to do that. Local congregations deal in particularities, made of particularly unique persons, in particularly unique communities, with particularly unique challenges.

God is asking us people who call the rural home the same question posed to Moses, "What's that in your hand?" (Exodus 4:1-5).

Only God can turn a stick into a snake. Only God can split a sea. But we play a particular role in God's plan. We lift the stick in the air when God tells us to. God is concerned about you and your congregation. God knows your name and the name of every person in your community.

God deals in somewhereness with somebodiness. You and your team will need to plough the fields of your local context and find the seeds of renewal for yourself. Fresh expressions of the rural church then result. Follow God's lead.

May you use your somebodiness to transform your somewhereness; and may the world never be the same.

Field Exercise

Somewhereness and Somebodiness Inventory

1. God gave Moses a stick, an asset, that God used to do miraculous things. What's in your hand? What is a key asset God has given you? How has God used it in the past?

2. Describe the "somebodiness" of your congregation: What is your identity? What is special about your identity?

3. Who are the people denied a sense of "somebodiness" in your context? Who is being treated unfairly or is marginalized? How might you form relationships with them?

4. What are some practices that might be useful in other churches but are not a fit with yours?

5. From reading or discussing this book, describe one idea for a fresh expression of church that you want to explore.

Field Story

Jacob Burson, Part-time Pastor, Emerson UMC, Emerson, Georgia: population 1,700

Emerson UMC is in a town just beyond the suburbs of Atlanta, Georgia. Our little community is divided up by the Etowah River, a mining operation, train tracks, a massive state-of-the-art sporting complex, Interstate 75, rolling foothills, and Georgia pine trees that shoot to the sky. For the locals, it's not the sporting complex that's the most significant landmark in town. That distinction belongs to Doug's Place, a "meat and three" restaurant that draws people from all over northwest Georgia for breakfast, lunch, and dinner. Directions to little Emerson UMC is easy. We tell folk who aren't sure where it is, "We're one block up the hill, behind Doug's Place." People seem to find us with those directions.

Just before the pandemic, our church explored the possibility of creating a dinner church. Just before COVID lockdowns started, we held our first dinner church gathering. We had more people packed into our basement fellowship hall for that gathering than we did on Sunday mornings. It felt like we had found something that would work for our little church. Then COVID changed everything. Our plans for a monthly dinner church gathering were put on hold, sort of.

During the initial months of COVID in 2020, our church partnered with other local churches to deliver meals to people in our community four days a week. This effort lasted three months, but it connected us to other churches, organizations, and dozens of people in the community. When the meal deliveries ended, we continued the fresh expression in our little church's parking lot, called "third Saturday." Our third Saturdays began with a partnership we made with a local food pantry from the Episcopal church, called the Red Door Food Pantry. On third Saturdays at our church, the Red Door Food Pantry drops off food pantry items that we then distribute to those in need who come to see us. We have also developed a partnership with a larger church nearby, Sam Jones Memorial UMC, which has a food truck. On third Saturdays, our friends from Sam Jones bring their food truck packed up with hot lunches their members prepared, which we distribute to the people who are served.

Emerson UMC worships with fewer than twelve people each Sunday. This third Saturday FX wouldn't be possible without the collaboration and partnership we have with other local churches and organizations. While our church is very small, we have something very significant: our facility and our location in the middle of the neighborhood. The only way a fresh expression is possible for a small rural church like ours is through partnerships and collaboration with other churches and organizations. The partnerships are crucial. While we may worship with twelve people on Sundays, on third Saturdays we have fifteen to twenty families who experience the love of God. We've built relationships with these people, we text each other, pray, have communion, deliver food to people who are shut in, and celebrate life with our new friends. Some of our new friends have even donated items from their food pantry bags to the little free pantry that we have on the front porch of the church parsonage. Love is contagious.

Fresh expressions are a phenomenal effort to connect people to new and engaging kingdom work, but it takes people who are willing to do things differently to get the ball rolling. In small and rural settings, it's very likely that to build a consistent fresh expression it will take collaboration with one or more other churches and organizations, pioneers, and outside-the-box thinkers. Once you all get together, the ideas begin to flow and even bigger dreams are shared.

I enjoy serving in the small and forgotten places. These places are considered "stepping stones" for many, but what if we dreamed for more from churches like Emerson UMC? What if we re-thought what these rural churches are capable of and positioned to do well? While we may not experience big crowds on Sundays, I'm certain heaven celebrates every time the hot-lunch plates are handed over along with every food bag loaded in the trunk.

Koinonia Liturgy

The Promise of Belonging

This liturgy was written by Tyler Kleeberger for use at The Farmhouse—a rural church trying to practice the principles covered in this book. Feel free to use or adapt this liturgy for your content. At the least, we hope this provides a valuable articulation of the hope of rural churches disclosed in this book.

We proclaim that life is a gift—that the divine breath of grace and love has been with us since our first breath. And we proclaim that everyone, including us, can be at the table—for we are sharers of this same gift.

To participate in the great retelling of the world, we embrace the journey of selflessness. Our path is one of descent: to give up our rights for the sake of our neighbors. We do not seek to be served but to serve. We do not live and make decisions based on what we want but what is best for our interdependent well-being with one another. We do not use others as objects for our gain, but we yearn to be in such relationships that nothing can stay the same.

We gladly pursue the good of one another.

We humbly recognize that we can keep learning, that we can keep pursuing change, and that we can become the only version of ourselves that we need to be. Our movement, our telos, is toward the center of divine fullness.

Therefore, we promise to do no harm—to resist evil and injustice in whatever forms they present themselves among us and to renounce all forms of brokenness, all measures of unhealth, and all ways that do not reflect the divine. We promise to do all the good we can—to bring peace and wholeness—to make God's dream for the world real in this place. We promise to follow the way of Messiah—to learn of Christ's nature and enact that reality more and more in everything we do.

We believe we are unfolding as human beings and building a better world—that our growth will bring forth transformation, that our creativity will bring forth authenticity, and that our roots will make the crucified love of Messiah expose what is possible. And we believe this kind of community begins by being real with each other—in our diversity, pursing unity; in our difference, pursuing integration; and in our wounds, pursuing healing. We yearn to let our scars tell our story, we embrace darkness so that we can move through it, and we acknowledge that we are better when we work together, for it is the triune dance of self-transcendent love.

We desire to be present together. We desire to participate in sacred belonging as neighbors. And we desire to share our lives and gifts—as God/Adonai has been generous to us, we hope to share that irrational generosity with the world around us.

We profess that all creatures, even all of creation, are sacred—and we seek to uphold their life; for the smallest denomination of health is the health of all things, together.

We do not seek to get our way but to give ourselves to the flourishing of all. And we believe this happens when we are broken and poured for the healing of the world.

We believe a healthy rural place, with a reimagined church, will put a dent in changing the world. We, therefore, exist to foster this health in our place through everything we do.

That our lives, our relationships, our families, our community, our social systems, our economy, our culture, and our ecosystem will be all they are created to be. That we will tell a different story in this humanity project, and that all things will continue on the holy adventure of being put back together again. May we love ourselves, our neighbors, and the God of the universe with every cell in our being, and may the world never be the same because we belong together in community, in koinonia, such as this.

Notes

Soil Map: Start Digging Here

1. Nathan O. Hatch, *The Democratization of American Christianity* (New Haven: Yale University Press, 1989), 97.

2. David W. Bebbington, "The Return of the Spirit: The Second Great Awakening," *Christianity Today*, issue 23, page 24; https://www.christianity today.com/history/issues/issue-23/return-of-spirit-second-great-awakening .html.

3. John H. Wigger, *American Saint: Francis Asbury and the Methodists* (New York: Oxford University Press, 2009), 315.

4. Charles Grandison Finney, *Autobiography of Charles G Finney* (1876).

5. Jeffrey Williams, *Religion and Violence in Early American Methodism: Taking the Kingdom by Force* (Bloomington, IN: Indiana University Press, 2010), 60.

6. Hatch, *Democratization*, 28.

7. Hatch, *Democratization*, 18.

8. Hatch, *Democratization*, 25.

9. Hatch, *Democratization*, 25–26.

10. Hatch, *Democratization*, 43.

11. Hatch, *Democratization*, 46

12. Hatch, *Democratization*, 69

13. William Bentley, *The Diary of William Bentley, D.D.* (Salem, MA, 1911), 3:65, 503, 515, 271.

14. Hatch, *Democratization*, 17

15. Hatch, *Democratization*, 88.

16. Hatch, *Democratization*, 89.

17. Wigger, American Saint, 2.

18. Nathan O. Hatch, "The Puzzle of American Methodism," *Church History* 63, no. 2 (1994): 177–78, https://doi.org/10.2307/3168586.

19. Hatch, "Puzzle," 178.

20. Williams, *Religion and Violence*, 55.

21. Hatch, "Puzzle," 178.

22. Wigger, *American Saint*, 9.

23. Lester Ruth, "The 'Church of the Horse,'" *Christian History* 114 (May 27, 2015): 12.

24. Wigger, *American Saint*, 9.

25. Wigger, *American Saint*, 9.

26. Hatch, "Puzzle," 179.

27. Hatch, "Puzzle," 179.

28. Hatch, *Democratization*, 21.

29. Hatch, *Democratization*, 24.

30. Hatch, "Puzzle," 179.

31. Hatch, "Puzzle," 178.

32. Stephen H. Webb, "Introducing Black Harry Hoosier: The History Behind Indiana's Namesake," *Indiana Magazine of History* 98, no. 1 (2002): 30–41, http://www.jstor.org/stable/27792357.

33. Webb, "Harry Hoosier," 33.

34. Ruth, "Church of the Horse," 16.

35. Webb, "Harry Hoosier," 33.

36. Francis Asbury, *The Journal and Letters of Francis Asbury,* ed. Elmer C. Clark, J. Manning Potts, and Jacob S. Payton, 3 vols. (Nashville, 1958), 3:341–45, 453.

37. Hatch, *Democratization,* 76.

38. Williams, *Religion and Violence,* 111.

39. Hatch, *Democratization,* 77.

40. Webb, "Harry Hoosier," 34.

41. The Hebrew Bible name for Ecclesiastes is *Qoheleth,* which means "Preacher" or "Teacher."

42. For an in-depth treatment of fresh expressions, see Michael Beck with Jorge Acevedo, *A Field Guide to Methodist Fresh Expressions* (Nashville: Abingdon Press, 2020).

Introduction: The State of Rural Places

1. We recognize that the largest populations of Indigenous and Black Americans are mostly located in predominantly rural states, according to the 2010 US Census. It is also worth noting that Native American and African American populations hold a much longer history in rural communities than European populations. The contemporary white-centric norm is relatively new to history.

2. Wanton S. Webb, *Webb's Historical, Industrial and Biographical Florida: Part I* (New York: W. S. Webb & Company, 1885), 104.

3. Tex Sample, *Working Class Rage: A Field Guide to White Anger and Pain* (Nashville: Abingdon Press, 2018), 26.

4. Amel Toukabri and Lauren Medina, "Latest City and Town Population Estimates of the Decade Show Three-Fourths of the Nation's Incorporated Places Have Fewer Than 5,000 People," Census.gov, May 21, 2020, https://www.census.gov/library/stories/2020/05/america-a-nation-of-small-towns.html.

5. Allen T. Stanton, *Reclaiming Rural: Building Thriving Rural Congregations* (Lanham: Rowman & Littlefield, 2021), 3.

1. The Hope of the Rural Church

1. IMDB, *The Truman Show*, https://www.imdb.com/title/tt0120382/.

2. For a more descriptive account of *shalom* within Jeremiah's prophecy, see Tyler Kleeberg and Rowland L. Smith, *Red Skies—Ecological Entanglement: A Preferential Option for Creation* (Wyoming: 100 Movements Publishing, 2022), 83–102.

2. Rethinking the Parish

1. Howard Thurman, *Jesus and the Disinherited* (Boston: Beacon Press, 2022), 14.

2. Webb, "Harry Hoosier," 39.

3. Beck with Acevedo, *Field Guide to Methodist Fresh Expressions*.

4. Arthur S. Wood, *The Burning Heart: John Wesley, Evangelist* (Minneapolis: Bethany Fellowship, 1978), 125–36.

5. Graham Cray, *Mission-Shaped Church: Church Planting and Fresh Expressions in a Changing Context* (New York: Seabury, 2010), 100.

6. Michael Moynagh, *Church in Life: Emergence, Ecclesiology and Entrepreneurship* (London, UK: SCM Press, 2017), 2.

3. Learning to Die Somewhere

1. For further exploration of this concept, see Tyler Kleeberger, *Learning to Die Somewhere: Marriage, Transience, and the Elusive Difficulty of Belonging*, November 16, 2021, https://tylerkleeberger.com/content/learning-to-die-somewhere.

2. "Arranged / Forced Marriage Statistics" Statistic Brain, www.statisticbrain.com.

3. For pastors choosing to serve in a connectional system with itineracy, the place for belonging, responsibility, accountability, and permanence is rooted in their annual conference. The conference, which has geographical boundaries and an evolving culture, is potentially just as much a home as any small town.

4. George W. Carver and Gary R. Kremer, *George Washington Carver in His Own Words* (Columbia: University of Missouri Press, 1987). BrainyQuote.com, BrainyMedia Inc, 2022, https://www.brainyquote.com/quotes/george_washington_carver_752548, accessed April 7, 2022.

5. Community Context—Region 6: Northwestern Ohio Synod Congregations: 35.4 percent rural; 42.4 percent small city or town (fewer than 50,000); 7.6 percent medium city and suburbs (50,000 to 260,000); 12.0 percent large city (259,000); 2.5 percent suburb of large city.

6. ELCA Form A—Summary of Congregational Statistics as of 12/31/2019.

4. Circles That Heal

1. See https://www.context.org/iclib/ic30/berry/.

2. Edward O. Wilson, *Biophilia* (Cambridge, MA: Harvard University Press, 1984).

3. Jenny Odell, *How to Do Nothing: Resisting the Attention Economy* (Brooklyn: Melville House, 2019), xvii.

4. John Wesley, "Catholic Spirit," *The Standard Sermons in Modern English*, K. C. Kinghorn, ed. (Nashville, 2002), 102.

5. Michael Moynagh and Michael Beck, *The 21st Century Christian: Following Jesus Where Life Happens.*

6. E. Stanley Jones, *Christ of the Indian Road* (Nashville: Abingdon Press, 1925).

6. Cultivating the Kingdom of God

1. William Temple, "Letter from the Archbishop of the West Indies" in *Theology*, vol 59, (1956).

7. Field Cred

1. Michael Beck, *Deep and Wild: Remissioning Your Church from the Outside In* (Franklin, TN: Seedbed Publishing, 2021).

2. Some of these thoughts are adapted from a blog series by Michael Adam Beck, https://michaeladambeck.com/blog-2/.

3. The nineteenth-century circuit riders had a life expectancy of thirty-nine years.

4. Nathan Moskowitz, "Tola the Judge: A New Midrashic Analysis," *Jewish Bible Quarterly* 43, no. 1 (January 2015): 17, https://jbqnew.jewishbible.org/assets/Uploads/431/jbq_431_moskowitztola.pdf.

5. Alcoholics Anonymous, *The Twelve Traditions*, https://www.aa.org /the-twelve-traditions.

6. Luther's Works, American Edition, 40:19.

7. To be sure, clergy pensions were started in the mid-twentieth century because pastors and families (who moved often without equity in a home) were literally starving and destitute after a lifetime of service.

8. Somewhereness and Somebodiness

1. Italics added. See https://singjupost.com/what-is-your-lifes -blueprint-by-dr-martin-luther-king-jr-full-transcript/?singlepage=1.

2. Stephen Webb notes Hosier was also spelled Hoosier, Hoshur, and Hossier ("Harry Hosier," 34).

3. Thomas Coke, *Extracts of the Journal of the Rev. Dr. Coke's Five Visits to America* (London: Printed by G. Paramore and sold by G. Whitfield, 1793), 18.

4. Webb, "Harry Hosier," 35.

5. Webb, "Harry Hosier," 35.

6. G. A. Raybold, *Reminiscences of Methodism in West Jersey* (New York: Lane and Scott, 1849), 166–67.

7. Thomas Coke, *Extracts*, 18.

8. Webb, "Harry Hoosier," 41.

9. Webb, "Harry Hosier," 36.

10. Webb, "Harry Hosier," 38.

11. Webb, "Harry Hosier," 39.

12. Webb, "Harry Hosier," 41.

13. Webb, "Harry Hosier," 41.

14. Wigger, *American Saint*, 149–53.

15. Quoted in Hatch, *Democratization*, 86.

16. Sample, *Working Class Rage*, 46–50.

17. Katherine Cramer, *The Politics of Resentment: Rural Consciousness in Wisconsin and the Rise of Scott Walker* (Chicago: University of Chicago Press, 2016), 5–6, 12.

References

Alcoholics Anonymous. *The Twelve Traditions*. https://www.aa.org/the-twelve
-traditions.

Bebbington, David W. "The Return of the Spirit: The Second Great Awakening."
Christian History, Issue 23, 24.

Beck, Michael. *Deep Roots, Wild Branches: Revitalizing the Church in the Blended
Ecology*. Franklin, TN: Seedbed Publishing, 2019.

———. *Deep and Wild: Remissioning Your Church from the Outside In*. Franklin,
TN: Seedbed Publishing, 2021.

Beck, Michael, with Jorge Acevedo. *A Field Guide to Methodist Fresh Expressions*.
Nashville: Abingdon Press, 2020.

Beck, Michael, and Rosario Picardo. *Fresh Expressions in a Digital Age: How the
Church Can Prepare for a Post Pandemic World*. Nashville: Abingdon, 2021.

Bentley, William, The Diary of William Bently, D.D., 4 vols. Salem, MA: Essex
Institute, 1911.

Carver, George W., and Gary R. Kremer. *George Washington Carver in His Own
Words*. Columbia: University of Missouri Press, 1987.

Cramer, Katherine. The Politics of Resentment: Rural Consciousness in Wisconsin
and the Rise of Scott Walker. Chicago: University of Chicago Press, 2016.

Cray, Graham. *Mission-Shaped Church: Church Planting and Fresh Expressions in a
Changing Context*. New York: Seabury, 2010.

Coke, Thomas. *Extracts of the Journal of the Rev. Dr. Coke's Five Visits to America*.
London, printed by G. Paramore and sold by G. Whitfield, 1793.

Finney, Charles Grandison. *Autobiography of Charles G Finney*. 1876. Bloomington,
MN: Bethany House, 1977.

Goodhew, David, Andrew Roberts, and Michael Volland. *Fresh!: An Introduction to Fresh Expressions of Church and Pioneer Ministry.* London: SCM Press, 2012.

Greenfield, Susan. *Mind Change: How Digital Technologies Are Leaving Their Mark on Our Brains.* New York: Random House, 2015.

Hatch, Nathan O. *The Democratization of American Christianity.* New Haven: Yale University Press, 1989.

———. "The Puzzle of American Methodism." *Church History* 63, no. 2 (1994): 175–89.

Jones, E. Stanley. *Christ of the Indian Road.* Nashville, Abingdon Press, 1925.

"Francis Asbury Pioneer of Methodism: America's Most Explosive Church Movement." *Christian History*, Issue 114.

King Martin Luther, Jr. https://singjupost.com/what-is-your-lifes-blueprint-by-dr-martin-luther-king-jr-full-transcript/?singlepage=1.

Loyer, Kenneth Milton. "'And to Crown All': John Wesley on Union with God in the New Creation." *Methodist Review* 1 (2009).

Mathews, Donald G. "Evangelical America—The Methodist Ideology" in *Perspectives on American Methodism*, edited by Russell E. Richey, Kenneth E. Rowe, and Joan Miller Schmidt, 29–30. Nashville: Kingswood, 1993.

Moynagh, Michael. *Church in Life: Emergence, Ecclesiology and Entrepreneurship.* London: SCM Press, 2017.

Moynagh, Michael, and Michael Beck. *The 21st Century Christian: Following Jesus Where Life Happens.* Harrington Interactive Media, 2021.

Moynagh, Michael, and Philip Harrold. *Church for Every Context: An Introduction to Theology and Practice.* London: SCM Press, 2012.

Nathan Moskowitz. "Tola the Judge: A New Midrashic Analysis." Jewish Bible Quarterly 43, no. 1 (January 2015): 17. https://jbqnew.jewishbible.org/assets/Uploads/431/jbq_431_moskowitztola.pdf.

Newbigin, Lesslie. *The Open Secret: An Introduction to the Theology of Mission.* Grand Rapids, MI: Eerdmans, 1995. Kindle.

Odell, Jenny. *How to Do Nothing: Resisting the Attention Economy.* Brooklyn: Melville House, 2019.

Plantinga, Cornelius. *Not the Way It's Supposed to Be: A Breviary of Sin.* Grand Rapids, MI: Eerdmans Publishing, 1996.

Raybold, G. A. *Reminiscences of Methodism in West Jersey.* New York: Lane and Scott, 1849.

Rohr, Richard. *The Universal Christ: How a Forgotten Reality Can Change Everything We See, Hope for, and Believe.* New York: Convergent Books, 2019.

Sample, Tex. *Working Class Rage: A Field Guide to White Anger and Pain.* Nashville: Abingdon Press, 2018.

Schmidt, Jean M. *Grace Sufficient: A History of Women in American Methodism, 1760–1939.* Nashville: Abingdon Press, 1999.

Stanton, Allen T. *Reclaiming Rural: Building Thriving Rural Congregations.* Lanham: Rowman & Littlefield, 2021.

Statistic Brain. "Arranged / Forced Marriage Statistics." www.statisticbrain.com.

Thurman, Howard. *Jesus and the Disinherited.* Boston: Beacon Press, 2022.

Toukabri, Amel, and Lauren Medina, "Latest City and Town Population Estimates of the Decade Show Three-Fourths of the Nation's Incorporated Places Have Fewer Than 5,000 People." Census.gov, May 21, 2020. https://www.census.gov/library/stories/2020/05/america-a-nation-of-small-towns.html.

Webb, Stephen H. "Introducing Black Harry Hoosier: The History Behind Indiana's Namesake." *Indiana Magazine of History* 98, no. 1 (2002): 30–41. http://www.jstor.org/stable/27792357.

Webb, Wanton S. *Webb's Historical, Industrial and Biographical Florida: Part I.* New York: W. S. Webb & Company, 1885.

Wesley, John, and Kenneth C. Kinghorn. The standard sermons in modern English. Nashville, TN: Abingdon Press, 2002. "The Scripture Way of Salvation," 187.

Wigger, John H. *American Saint: Francis Asbury and the Methodists.* New York: Oxford University Press, 2009.

Williams, Jeffrey. *Religion and Violence in Early American Methodism: Taking the Kingdom by Force.* Bloomington, IN: Indiana University Press, 2010.

Wilson, Edward O. *Biophilia.* Cambridge, MA: Harvard University Press, 1984.

Wood, Arthur S. *The Burning Heart: John Wesley, Evangelist.* Minneapolis: Bethany Fellowship, 1978.